Conf
of a F
Ghost Hunter

M000305475

"Fascinating reading. How refreshing to meet a ghost hunter who doesn't crave the limelight but honestly helps people. We learn that not all ghost hunting is nice and simple!"

PHYLLIS GALDE, EDITOR IN CHIEF OF
FATE MAGAZINE

"Von Braschler offers us expert guidance and an insightful, personal narrative of his work with spirits and other energetic entities. This is an excellent read for those seeking a balanced and nuanced perspective on a too-often glamorized topic."

ANNA CARIAD-BARRETT, DMIN, MFT, COAUTHOR OF
SACRED MEDICINE OF BEE, BUTTERFLY, EARTHWORM, AND SPIDER

"Von Braschler's new book is a fascinating account of his experiences as a ghost hunter. It's an absorbing, compelling, authoritative look at this fascinating subject by a renowned expert in the field."

RICHARD WEBSTER, AUTHOR OF
PSYCHIC PROTECTION FOR BEGINNERS

"Von Braschler's firsthand accounts of confrontations with human ghosts and nonhuman spirits throw new light on the afterlife and our mysterious relationship to it. His often terrifying quest for the truth connecting this world with the next amounts to nothing less than a voyage of discovery no reader will ever forget."

FRANK JOSEPH, AUTHOR OF
BEFORE ATLANTIS AND *GODS OF THE RUNES*

Confessions of a Reluctant Ghost Hunter

A Cautionary Tale of Encounters
with Malevolent Entities
and Other Disembodied Spirits

Von Braschler

Destiny Books
Rochester, Vermont • Toronto, Canada

Destiny Books
One Park Street
Rochester, Vermont 05767
www.DestinyBooks.com

Destiny Books is a division of Inner Traditions International

Library of Congress Cataloging-in-Publication Data

Braschler, Von, 1947–
  Confessions of a reluctant ghost hunter : a cautionary tale of encounters with malevolent entities and other disembodied spirits / Von Braschler.
      pages cm
  Includes bibliographical references and index.
  ISBN 978-1-62055-382-4 (pbk.) — ISBN 978-1-62055-383-1 (e-book)
  1. Braschler, Von, 1947– 2. Parapsychology—Biography. 3. Ghosts—Research.
I. Title.
  BF1027.B64A3 2014
  133.1—dc23
                                                                    2014001294

Printed and bound in the United States by Versa Press, Inc.

10 9 8 7 6 5 4 3 2 1

Text design by Priscilla Baker and layout by Debbie Glogover
This book was typeset in Garamond Premier Pro with ITC American Typewriter Std as display font

To send correspondence to the author of this book, mail a first-class letter to the author c/o Inner Traditions • Bear & Company, One Park Street, Rochester, VT 05767, and we will forward the communication.

*Dedicated to the survivors of these
deadly encounters.
You know who you are.*

Contents

Foreword by Jim Harold   ix

Note to Reader   xiii

Introduction: I Am Ready to Tell My Story   1

1   Early Ghosts I Have Known   6

2   Meeting My Ghost-Hunting Teacher   30

3   Helen's Ghost-Hunting Instructions   44

4   Ghost Hunting at an Old Portland Church   57

5   Mutilations, Floating Heads, and a Talking Dead Girl   70

6   Dealing with the Spirits in My House   85

7   The Herbalist's Haunted Trailer in the Forest   100

8   Confronting the Spirit in the Trailer   113

9   Returning the Spirit Back to the Trailer   129

10   Consequences of the Trailer Haunting   143

11   The Unseen Problems with Ghosts and Hauntings   159

12   Some Dos and Don'ts for Ghost Hunters   167

Recommended Reading   171

Index   172

Foreword

If you watch TV, listen to talk radio, or use the Internet, you might think that ghost hunting is as casual a pursuit today as bowling was years ago. Paranormal groups are popping up across our cultural landscape as quickly as the manufacturers of electronics can market assorted gizmos to them, to capture various phenomena during their late-night investigations.

What training is required to hang up one's shingle as a ghost hunter and spirit specialist? Well, it's on a par with what was required to declare oneself a physician in the old West. That is to say, no training whatsoever. Get a black T-shirt (with an obligatory logo) and a digital recorder, and most people will think you're fully equipped to delve successfully into the most important spiritual mysteries in existence today.

What's the harm, you might ask? Isn't it all in good fun? After all, no one gets hurt, right? We scare ourselves a bit, go home, and continue on with our lives.

In this book, Von Braschler reminds us that ghost hunting and attempts to communicate with the dead are not necessarily all fun and games. He asserts that forays into the affairs of human and nonhuman spirits can have very real consequences. Even if the endeavor involved is as innocent as asking deceased Aunt Martha for the secret ingredient in her apple pie, forces that we don't understand can be unleashed.

These forces can create extreme mental, spiritual, and physical harm to the living—not to mention the impacts on the spirits themselves. After reading this book, one is reminded of Nietzsche's quote, "And when you gaze long into an abyss, the abyss also gazes into you."

Many readers may disagree with Von Braschler's final conclusions regarding the need for caution when practicing ghost hunting and spirit seeking. I'm not sure that I even completely agree with him. What I *will* say is that he has a lot of experience to draw from and, given that he himself once rushed in where fools fear to tread, his interested followers would be wise to heed his uttered words of cautionary wisdom.

Von Braschler brings up a number of important points, some of which I hadn't pondered until now. If the human spirits we encounter are human spirits, they deserve respect. Should we be interrupting their rest just because it makes *us* feel better? Is that really ethical? If they are nonhuman spirits, are we inviting in forces that are capable of wreaking all matter of real-world havoc? Are we stirring a pot that might boil over and burn us in very unanticipated and unpredictable ways?

These and other important questions are asked in *Confessions of a Reluctant Ghost Hunter.* Buckle up for a ride that will chill you down to your bones but will also make you ponder the mysteries of life in a way that you probably never have before. Reading this book is a very worthwhile journey, and one that any person interested in paranormal affairs should undertake.

Jim Harold

Jim Harold is America's most popular paranormal podcaster, with a loyal following that spans the globe. For years he has had a love affair with the strange, the supernatural, and the unexplained. The Paranormal Podcast and Jim Harold's Campfire are regularly among the top podcasts in their categories on iTunes, often outranking mainstream media programming. You can also find his programs at jimharold.com and on Roku and TuneInRadio. Jim became a published author with his 2011 book, *Jim Harold's Campfire: True Ghost Stories,* and a sequel to that book, *True Ghost Stories: Jim Harold's Campfire 2,* published in 2013. He lives in northeastern Ohio.

Note to Reader

This is essentially a true ghost story, or series of ghost stories, that consumed my life and the lives of some of my friends in the 1980s. The story begins in the San Juan Islands and ends on Mount Hood in Oregon. On this mountain I had three difficult encounters with spirits that I initially had assumed were ghosts of deceased people, but have come to believe might have involved spirits other than ghosts.

I should confess to you that I have changed a few things in the narration, which doesn't really alter the story in any significant way. For instance, I might have changed a name, date, or location slightly in reporting the hauntings in order to protect the privacy of the people involved.

If any details in this book appear to the actual people in the story to be slightly inaccurate or switched, I apologize in advance and request your indulgence. It was only my attempt to tell the real story as starkly and directly as possible, without intrusion into anyone's life or past.

Thanks to all of you for your contributions to this book. To those of you whose lives are still vexed by the accounts reported, you have my deepest concern and best wishes for a brighter tomorrow.

VON BRASCHLER

I Am Ready to Tell My Story

I had always thought that ghosts were basically playful and harmless spirits of people who had passed away but never totally left us. Like many people who are sensitive psychically, I have often been able to notice ghosts. Oh, I could not always *see* them plainly, but I could *sense* when they were around; and quite often I could verify that my detections were spot-on. However, despite the fact that I could detect the ghosts, I never knew quite what to do with them or how to interact with them. I just saw them as a curiosity and pretty much ignored them as unimportant trappings that came with some buildings that had a troubled past. And I always assumed that ghosts were nothing more than the playful and harmless spirits of people who had passed on but had never totally left us.

Then one day I met a professional named Helen who visited haunted houses on request and effectively communicated with ghosts, convincing them to leave. She told me about her successes and the easy steps she seemed to follow to extricate confused and even stubborn interlopers from the spirit realm. She made ghost busting sound easy enough that I wanted to try it; so she walked me through it during two sit-down sessions. I returned home and decided that I was up to the task, should anyone ever report a haunting to me and request that I intervene with their ghosts on site.

Some things appear simpler than they truly are, of course. There are complexities involved with trying to contact spirits that go bump in the night, as I quickly found out. When I returned from the San Juan Islands where I met the ghost hunter Helen at the Outlook Inn, I tried contacting various ghosts to encourage them to depart the location they had chosen to haunt. I assumed that these ghosts would be easy to connect with and with little or no trouble I would be able to convince them to leave.

These were my first big mistakes.

I quickly learned that in some situations I was badly outmatched.

In the past (prior to meeting Helen) I had slept in a haunted hotel in London, lived in a triplex apartment in Seattle where a wandering soul had committed suicide. I had also experienced the spirit of my deceased cat jumping onto my bed to sleep with me at night. I had spoken to my dad after he died and been startled by a Native American who popped into my living room and just as quickly popped out again. In addition, I had actually convinced ghostly presences known only by their carved graffiti on the chimney as "The Order" to relocate from my attic. So I was not afraid of ghostly spirits.

All of that changed when, after having been trained by Helen, I began to ghost hunt in the haunted buildings of Oregon during the early 1980s. That was when I learned what fear of the unknown is all about. That was when I learned about the dangers of trying to extricate spirits from haunted buildings, spirits that did not want to leave. We came to realize in time that not all of the spirits who haunted buildings were ghosts of deceased people but were probably spirits of quite a different sort. They proved much harder to handle. My teacher had warned me about some of them. I came to learn that there were more things out there to fear.

One can hardly blame my teacher for the problems that I later encountered. She was very proficient at contacting ghosts and gently convincing them to move on. She taught me a few simple tricks and described tools that I could bring to a haunting that would help to convince stubborn ghosts that it was time to move on. She normally was able to charm the deceased to leave. In her experience, they were normally confused or simply reluctant to depart.

Once again, my friends and I encountered something more than simple ghosts on Mount Hood; and the interaction with these spirits was not that tame or cordial. I confess at the same time that I do not claim to be as charming or persuasive as my instructor, Helen.

My first story involves a large, old church in Portland where a ghost had reportedly roamed the building for many years and was noticed by many people.

The second ghost story involves the disappearance of a girl who visited a cabin in the woods and then called her sister from beyond the grave. This story is interwoven with the ghostly presence of floating heads of spirits that haunted my house at the same time that the girl disappeared and mysterious animal mutilations were occurring on Mount Hood.

The third story takes place in a mobile home near the town of Rhododendron in the area of the Mount Hood National Forest. Here dogs died mysteriously, a spirit that resembled a little girl with golden curls played, and people were choked in their sleep.

There are several other ghost stories in this narrative, and all of them are true. As a lifelong journalist, I have tried to tell the story as accurately and clearly as possible, reporting to you exactly what happened.

If I have intruded into the lives of some friends and neighbors in the telling of these stories and told too much or missed something, I apologize. I might have changed a name, date, or small detail here or there, but you have in your hands the true account of what happened to me and my neighbors back in the 1980s.

I also want to dispel any conjecture you may have, as you read these encounters with spirits, that the friends and neighbors who came up against these spirits were in any way part of the problem. These were good people in impossibly difficult situations. They didn't bring this torment upon themselves. They were innocents caught in a web.

Those of us who lived through these events are pleased to be around to tell our stories. Not all of us were so fortunate. Some of the survivors went on to suffer major painful disruptions in their lives. These hellish encounters with deadly spirits were so disruptive to my *own* life that I suppressed them for a long time, choosing not to write about them until now. In the meantime I wrote self-help books about consciousness development, time perception, dream work, and healing.

As you read the accounts of these intense battles with unseen spirits, you might think that I have exaggerated to make the stories seem more exciting than they really were. Rest assured, that is not the case. Rather, I have tried to report the stories in the order that they occurred and as simply as possible. The reporting needs no embellishment.

I now present for my readers a how-to primer on contacting and dealing with ghosts, along with a warning about the dangers involved. It is important to remember that not every haunting will be simply contacting the lost spirit of somebody's dead aunt who is confused or reluctant to move on. The spirits who from time to time haunt our homes and buildings can prove to be much more difficult and dangerous. Be warned. It's not always as fun and innocent as some of the ghost stories you might see on television.

However, given that we seem to be going through the biggest craze in ghost hunting and spiritual contact since the spiritualist movement of the 1930s, people need to realize that disturbing spirits and hunting them down can lead to some dark confrontations without easy resolution. Although these endeavors might appear interesting on the face of things, they need to be taken seriously and treated with the utmost respect.

Since these encounters with spirits in Oregon, I have continued to see ghosts. I have chosen not to serve as ghost hunter, however, and have not offered my services to others in helping to contact and release spirits in homes or other buildings. Yes, I still discover them rather often and find it easy to sense their presence here and there. Occasionally I acknowledge them personally. Since my ghost-hunting days I have even encouraged spirits to leave a house that I occupied or encouraged them to make friendly adjustments to make themselves more scarce. I recognize now that some spirits just don't want to leave and cannot be convinced to leave entirely. But if they do no harm, I can live with them to a degree. But my years of actively hunting down ghosts in the homes of other people are over. I know the basics of how to contact them and encourage them to leave, but now know the dark side to stalking spirits as well.

And so, this is my own first-person story about ghost hunting and its unforeseen pitfalls. I am indebted to many people for their roles in these encounters. But my story would not be complete without a sincere note of thanks to my publisher, who had the courage to publish a book that is somewhat outside the range of typical "how-to" books on ghost hunting or stories about haunted houses, and decidedly darker than other books that I have submitted for publication.

1
Early Ghosts
I Have Known

I'll always remember how excited and hopeful I felt about being trained to find ghosts that haunted houses. I wanted to help them move along to the spirit realm and leave this physical world behind. It seemed so natural . . . so easy. I had a wonderful teacher who had successfully helped many people remove ghosts from their haunts simply by communicating with them and convincing them that hanging around was no longer in their best interest. My teacher showed me various ways to remove ghosts once I'd found them.

Based on her own happy stories of resolution, I wasn't prepared for the problems I would encounter when I tried this on my own. I blame no one for my bad experiences. Instead, I recognize that I failed to realize the complexities involved with haunted buildings and the variety of spirits I might encounter in them.

But I'm getting ahead of my story here.

Everybody comes to the murky world of ghost hunting with some bit of history and past orientation. Hopefully, that previous experience helps prepare them for what they may encounter when things get a little crazy. For full disclosure, I would like to share with you my early background with ghosts.

My earliest experiences with spirits and haunted buildings were enough to raise a few hairs. I tell you this to underscore the fact that I was no babe in the woods when it came to dealing with haunted houses. But I must add that my early experiences were pretty tame compared to what I would later encounter. As I state in the introduction to this book, I'd always assumed that what I perceived as a ghostly presence was simply a person who had died and failed to fully move on. I had also assumed that the spirits I encountered were essentially benevolent and posed no real danger to me or anyone else.

After actively attempting to deal with ghostly presences and forcefully remove spirits, however, I was shocked to encounter some very difficult spirits, which proved that my early assumptions about ghosts were erroneous. I began to find haunted buildings where I came up against spirits that were not merely the simple spirits of people who had died.

Spirits can be deceptive and devious. They can pose as something they're not. One might present itself as the ghost of dear old Aunt Sally or some old man who once lived in your home and now hides in its walls and crawl spaces, wandering out only at night. But you might not be seeing them as they truly are.

They can be manipulative and bothersome. They also can try to kill you if you give them half a chance. Whether these dangerous spirits are common or rare, I can't say. I can only report my own experiences as a trained ghost hunter who came dangerously close to losing his life in an attempt to remove a so-called ghost from a house.

In the following pages I'll recount to you my earliest encounters with things that go bump in the night. I'm certain you'll agree that, compared to my later experiences, these were relatively sweet and tender encounters. In them I observed what were no doubt departed spirits that were simply confused to find themselves hanging around this physical world when their physical form had died.

THE NEWSROOM GHOST

While employed in 1979 as a publisher for the *Sandy Post,* a small newspaper on Mount Hood, I discovered that our printing plant, located in the town of Gresham, was haunted. The ghostly encounters that I was privy to seemed to happen late at night, close to midnight, when I was the only person in the big, empty, cement building. I would be puttering away, getting things ready for the next day's edition of the paper, when I would hear the strange noises of a ghost that left little doubt that he was out and about.

The first instance occurred in the summer, when I would typically be working in the air-conditioned lunchroom. Given that I was the only one around, I could spread my things out on the large lunch tables. The rest of the building consisted of the composition and press areas, which lay behind heavy doors to the back of the building, and a large combined newsroom and business area in an open room at the front of the building, just outside the lunchroom.

My newsroom ghost made its presence known to me on three separate nights.

The first night I was startled to hear the doors that block the pressroom slam shut. These were very large metal doors at the back of the composition area near the big presses and were heavy and hard to open for a reason: they buffered the noise of the presses. They also deterred folks from wandering back into that area when the high-speed presses were running. Given all this, it was very unlikely that the doors had been merely left ajar or had blown shut by a strange draft. It took a strong press operator, using both hands, to open and close the pressroom doors.

When I heard the noise I naturally ran to investigate it, even though I could easily identify the sound as that of the heavy doors slamming shut; it was that distinctive. Although I knew what the sound itself was, whatever had caused the doors to open and close was a mystery. Of course, I found nobody in the pressroom or in the composition area. Both areas were dark and empty. I was the only soul around and the building was deathly quiet.

A strange chill ran up my spine and made the hair on the back of my neck tingle. There was no earthly explanation for what might have caused the mysterious sound. Was the building haunted?

I gathered up my things quickly, returned to the lunchroom and turned off the lights, and left the newspaper plant. I didn't bother to look around. I didn't want to see or hear anything else inside the building that night.

The same thing happened the following week. Again, I found myself behind on my week's work and struggling to get the next paper out on time. I really wasn't expecting another scare. Nonetheless, I decided to try to hurry through my tasks and get out earlier that night. But my evening stay grew longer and longer, and soon there I was, working alone in the newspaper plant close to midnight. I was so absorbed in what I was doing that I didn't think about the consequences of a repeat encounter with the ghost. After all, nothing had really happened to me the first time. I had merely heard a weird noise that I couldn't explain. I hadn't expected something so strange to happen twice.

Not twice to the same person, right?

Wrong.

At about a quarter to midnight I heard what sounded like typing coming from one of the old typewriters in the business area in the front of the building. Our bookkeepers still used old Underwood manuals, given that only the newsroom was computerized back then. Thus I easily recognized the sound of the old Underwood typewriter and someone pounding its keys. They were pounding the keys in a concerted way that sounded like serious typing. There was a regular rhythm and pace to it, as though the words came easily to the typist. Whoever was typing knew how to type.

When I tell this story, people always ask me *what* the ghost typed. That's a reasonable question. To find out the answer, all I had to do was go to the front desk and check the typewriter. Even if there was no paper in its spindle, the depression of the keys would certainly have left an impression on the rubber roller itself.

But the truth is I *didn't* investigate. After hearing the sound, I quickly grabbed my papers and keys and left the building. I didn't want to meet the ghost up close and personal.

Unfortunately, though, I had no choice in the matter. A few weeks later I found myself working late and alone at the plant again. This time, however, I decided that I would close the doors to the lunchroom and get my work done as quickly as possible in order to leave the building as soon as I could. And the plan seemed to work. I wasn't distracted at all, and at around 11:00 p.m., I gathered my things to leave.

Just as I was departing the lunchroom, however, I caught sight of something out of the corner of my eye. There was no door to the composition room, and I could easily see back there even though the lighting was dim. At one of the typography machines where compositors set type for display ads I saw the hunched-over figure of what looked like a wiry old man. He wore one of those green shades on his head, the sort of visors that old typesetters used to wear in the early days of the newspaper business. He was absorbed in his work and seemed oblivious to my presence.

I couldn't get out of that building fast enough.

Later, people asked me why I didn't try to communicate with the ghost of the newspaper building. Well, I had no idea what I might say to him or what he might say to me. It was easier to avoid a confrontation entirely.

That old newspaper ghost didn't seem dangerous, but he certainly had made himself known.

THE DROWNED COMPOSITOR

On a Sunday morning a month or two later, I walked into the vacant building again, thinking I'd be all alone. I remember it was almost fall, and the building felt a bit cold. Upon entering it, I walked into the composing room because I felt like looking around, just in case the old ghost was still back there setting type.

I was about to flick on the lights when an odd feeling came over me. I hadn't seen anything ghostly, but one page of a newspaper hung on a far wall of the room. It was covered with photos that ordinarily do not clutter the walls at that location, which was strange in itself. And the clipping hadn't hung there the day before. Why would anybody come down to the plant on a Sunday morning to hang up a newspaper clipping? I also realized that the clipping wasn't from one of our publications; it was headline news that had been ripped out of our competing newspaper's Sunday edition.

The only light in the room was that of a hallway light spilling over into the room and thus I couldn't ascertain what the article and its photographs were all about. But two strong images filled my head as I stared at the paper. The first image was of one of my friends, a young woman who set type in that very room. In fact, I had just seen her and spoken with her late Friday afternoon. In my mind's eye I saw her drowning in the Columbia River. Beside her was the image of a capsized boat. These were strong impressions that came to me out of nowhere.

I flicked on the lights and walked across the room, feeling scared deep inside. I had a horrible feeling that the clipping on the wall held bad news. And, yes, the story was a report of a boat that had capsized on the Columbia River the day before. The boat had been undergoing tests of its new steering equipment, which had malfunctioned. A woman was below deck when the boat flipped over and apparently had remained alive for a little while before drowning. She was one of several friends of the owner of the boat and had simply joined them for a ride.

That woman was my friend from the newsroom.

My friend sometimes worked on weekends when production at the plant fell behind, and although I didn't see her in the newsroom that Sunday morning, I had clearly felt her ghostly presence there.

I believe her spirit visited me that Sunday morning in the newsroom.

GHOST CATS

I had a kitten that was too young to go outside, but one hot summer afternoon I left the front door open so she could go out on the porch to play. I remember I was watching the classic movie *National Velvet,* which is about a girl's love for a horse, and thinking about how wonderful it is to grow up with a pet one can bond with.

My kitten, named Itty Bitty Kitty, wanted to go outside to play and fully explore the wonders of the pleasant afternoon. She liked to romp on the big front porch and bat the rope that dangled from one side of the porch pillars. I had played with her out there in days past, and she had never strayed from the porch while I was with her.

On this day, however, Itty Bitty Kitty decided to explore. She left the porch and front lawn, and shortly thereafter two boys knocked on my door and said that my kitten was in the road. I ran outside and found her mangled body in the storm drain on the far side of the street, where apparently she had dragged herself in the hope of finding refuge. Her dead body was still warm. Minutes before, it had held her life.

But her presence at my house didn't end with her death. For a couple of weeks, at daybreak, I would see her playing in the backyard, where she would be darting between flowers and the rocks of my terraced garden. I don't think she fully realized that she'd died. Clearly, she was unprepared to move on from this world.

And Itty Bitty was not my only pet who haunted me after death.

Miss Polly, a Rose Point Siamese, was a twenty-one-year-old cat who loved to sleep on my bed. She developed cancer of the mouth, which was discovered when the vet was cleaning her teeth. That cancer soon spread to her brain. Realizing that her end was near, I provided her with home hospice care. The night she died, she tried to climb onto my bed when I retired, as she usually did. She couldn't negotiate the jump, however, and lay dying on the floor. So I carried her up to the bed, where she died peacefully, looking into my eyes as she did so.

But her nightly habit of hopping up onto the foot of my bed was apparently a habit that she was not willing to surrender. For the next couple of weeks, I felt something hop onto the foot of my bed every night. It was easy to tell she was there—you can easily tell when something plops onto a bed where you are peacefully and gently reclining. Sometimes in the morning I would even detect a familiar cat odor and a slight indentation at the foot of my bed. For a family of cats, cuddling to sleep together is a natural part of belonging to a pride. When a cat enters your home, you adopt it as a part of your family and it adopts you as part of its pride.

After a couple of weeks, I no longer felt my cat's presence at night. I concluded that Miss Polly had finally moved on. Perhaps she felt that enough time had passed, and I would be able to carry on without her.

THE LONDON HOTEL GHOST

When a publisher sent me to London to attend a book fair one spring, I stayed in a very old townhouse that had been converted into a guesthouse. It was one of those tall, narrow buildings that is hundreds of years old. One of its features was a spiral staircase, the tiny landings of which, on each of the building's seven floors, opened to the guest rooms on that particular floor. When I checked into the hotel, I was given keys to room 7, which was on the top floor of the building.

At first glance room 7 looked fairly normal. It was small, with space for scarcely more than a bed and a clothes closet. An overhead light adorned the ceiling, and although there was a sink in the bedroom the room shared a water closet and claw-footed bathtub with another guest room down the hall.

When I first set foot in room 7, I was ready to rest, recover from my jet lag, and otherwise settle in. The place seemed very quiet and peaceful, and I felt happy to be alone there. First impressions can be deceiving, however, especially when one is in a foreign place. Shortly after nodding off I was startled by the sound of running water. The faucet in the sink was running. It was not running full blast, but it was definitely emitting more than a trickle. I was certain that had not been the case when I had retired—in fact, I hadn't used the sink at all.

I lay awake in bed thinking about that oddity and wondering how the water faucet had turned itself on. Everything was still and quiet in the room except for the sound of the water; I could hear nothing outside in the hall.

Suddenly, out of nowhere, a little laugh broke the night's silence. Had I really heard correctly?

Nervously, I bounded out of bed and turned off the faucet. I returned to bed and lay quietly, fully awake, and surrounded by silence once more.

As though to tease me, the water began to run from the faucet again. As before, it was much more than a drip, but not a full blast of water. Again, I heard the same laughter.

Realizing that I was probably in the presence of a ghost with a gift for practical jokes, I turned over in bed without much concern.

"Okay, okay!" I said out loud. "Very funny. I get it. Now let me get some sleep, if you don't mind."

From that point on, all of the hijinks stopped.

The next morning I told the desk clerk that I had experienced some odd things the previous night in my room. I described the events in detail.

"Oh, you must be in room 7," she said quickly, nodding. Enough said.

Another guest overheard us. "Room 7, right? Yes, I've been in that room before. Fun and games, eh?"

Curiously, I heard no more running water or laughter on subsequent nights inside of room 7.

DAD'S FINAL GOOD-BYE

My dad was sort of a sentimental guy. He was definitely a man who loved his family. Unfortunately, he suffered a massive heart attack at the age of forty-seven and was forced to retire prematurely at the age of forty-eight. He spurned the triple bypass surgery that the doctors recommended but agreed to cut back on his smoking habit by smoking only one pack of cigarettes a day, instead of his usual three.

At this point in his life he became a sort of suburban rancher, looking after two horses and mending wooden fences all day when he was not otherwise busy pruning trees or working on machinery. His ailing heart caught up with him at the age of sixty-three. One morning, when he started to stand up to greet the day, he fell down and died, with one shoe on and the other shoe off.

But apparently he wanted to hang around a little bit longer.

One night I had a very vivid dream. It featured bright colors, which was unlike my typical dreams. In this one I was sitting on a sofa in my father's house, and I realized that I had just popped into this scene in a somewhat awkward way—as if I had been abruptly placed there for some specific reason. While sitting on the sofa, I started thinking about my dad, since he'd just died. At that moment I heard a sound down the hall, and then saw my father stick his head playfully around the corner of the hallway, as if to surprise me.

"But I thought you were dead!" I said to him. "How can this be?"

He smiled at me playfully. "I think we've played a trick on you," he said. "I'm not dead. But *somebody* is."

I just stared at him. "No!" I said. "I'm sure *you* were the one who died. You had me going there for a minute, though."

"Gotcha!" he chirped. And then he disappeared before my eyes.

I sat there for a minute before realizing I wasn't really in that room, and that I was dreaming. Then I instantly woke up—with these images fresh in my mind.

I've since heard similar stories from many other people, leading me to believe that our dead friends and relatives occasionally drop by just after they die to touch base or say good-bye.

DEB'S PINK RIBBON

I had a roommate who liked to sew. She also enjoyed her cat. Deb was a cancer survivor—someone with a terminal brain tumor who had lost all of her hair, prepared to die, and then underwent an amazing remission. The story of her miraculous recovery had been published in various medical books, and she had also appeared on radio to discuss it.

Deb credited her long-haired black cat, Wizard, with her recovery, given that he had stood by her side throughout her whole agonizing ordeal. He was always with her, and Deb said that Wizard sent her energy and returned her to health.

Years later Deb and her cat were living at my house, and Deb was going to work every day. Twice a year she'd visit a health clinic to make sure the cancer hadn't returned. One day, however, she was too sick to go in to work. She stumbled while trying to walk upstairs to her bedroom. Some of her friends and I performed an intervention, convincing her to go to the hospital. Soon thereafter we learned that her brain tumor had returned, and the cancer was spreading rapidly.

Going through Deb's things to collect some of her personal items to bring to the hospital, I discovered a recent clinical report that suggested Deb might have failed to get a CAT scan during her last visit, which might have detected the tumor before it spread. Thinking back, Deb probably sensed the return of the tumor and was in denial.

Deb faded fast. Her cat sat at home this time, while she went through the hospital treatments. The corrective measures the hospital tried were too little too late. When Deb found herself in a hospice awaiting death at the age of thirty-two, I brought her black cat to visit her. Wizard would perch on her bed, or, when Deb was in her wheelchair, Wizard would sit on her lap. There he would remain, loyally at her side. During these visits, he purred more loudly than I've ever heard a cat purr. Deb, who didn't have much outward, physical expression at this point, would manage to smile and pet Wizard as best she could, although it was difficult for her, due to her illness, to move her hands and arms very much.

On the morning that Deb died, the phone in my house rang; Deb was gone. I lay down for a moment, and, in my mind's eye, I clearly saw Deb tiptoeing down the steps of the house to the living room. I saw her walk barefoot across the carpet and crouch down to play with her cat.

She was dangling a long pink ribbon in the air for Wizard to swipe and bat around. Then I watched her pet the cat with one hand while turning to drop the ribbon into a wicker basket. The long ribbon fluttered as it dropped slowly into the basket. Then Deb disappeared.

This was such a startling and lucid image that I sprang to my feet and dashed downstairs. Indeed, her black cat was sitting in the living room. Nearby, in the corner, was the small wicker basket where we kept all of Wizard's toys. I looked into the basket and inside it, on top of everything, lay a long pink ribbon that I'd never seen before. I later discovered a lot of pink ribbons and a sewing pattern in the hall closet. Here Deb had secretly been storing notions with which to make gifts, presumably for the Christmas she would never celebrate. I left these sewing materials untouched for some time because it seemed that Deb might want access to them.

Other evidence of Deb's presence abounded. On many evenings the stereo or television in her former bedroom would seem to turn itself on. I would leave it to play by itself for quite a while, returning hours later to turn it off. Deb had loved my old Victorian house. Was she returning to it after she'd died because she missed it so much?

In time, Deb's family came to collect all of her things. After that, I never heard from Deb again—but I bet her cat did.

A MESSAGE FROM "THE ORDER"

Eventually I moved away from the house I had shared with Deb, and when I did, I took Wizard with me.

We moved into another hundred-year-old Victorian house with an attic, which I decided to remodel by adding an additional bedroom to it. Certain spirits had other ideas, however. After I had plastered and painted the attic's walls, fixed up closets inside the exposed crawl spaces, and finished and carpeted the new bedroom, I noticed markings on some of the chimney bricks that poked through the third floor from a fireplace on the second floor below. The markings appeared to have been written in black marking pen (appearances can be deceiving).

In printed letters, the black markings spelled out "The Order." Assuming this was just some old scribbling with markers, I started to rub the words out, using a rag that had been soaked in soapy water. That did nothing. So I tried a stronger cleaning solvent and a scrub brush. I scrubbed a long time before the dark printing seemed to fade. I hadn't totally removed the markings, but after some serious scrubbing, they weren't as noticeable as they had been before.

The next day, however, I was shocked to see that the same markings were darker and bolder than ever. Scrubbing even harder, I was nonetheless unable to make them fade. I tried again the following day and finally determined that no amount of scrubbing would make the markings go away completely. The dark letters had somehow been etched or carved into the brick, and they were black as black could be.

"The Order". . . Who had written this message, and what could it possibly mean? I began to think it was a name that the writers of the message called themselves; an organization of sorts.

I also felt that it was somehow important to them that I knew they were there, as though they had staked out a marked claim to this space in the attic. And now I had moved into their space and had turned it into a bedroom. Did they feel crowded out? Threatened? I didn't know how to locate them, communicate with them, or reason with them. Of course, I wanted them to leave, preferably before somebody moved into the new bedroom and found them and their ominous message.

At that time I knew nothing about communicating with spirits and removing them from haunted houses, so I looked up the word "banishing" to try to find a way to remove them. I settled on a ritual called "the Lesser Banishing Ritual of King Solomon." This simple ritual is a form of high magick, but it's easy enough so that one doesn't have to be a magician or a versed practitioner of high magick to perform it.

I tried it and the markings on the bricks finally disappeared completely. Furthermore, no one has ever mentioned anything odd about the room, even when I've dropped hints to that effect. So I guessed that "The Order" had moved on.

But where did it go?

In my banishing ritual I had ordered it deeper into the crawl space of the attic and away from the opening to the crawl space itself, where the inhabitants of the new room had begun hanging their clothes on bars I installed for that purpose. Boxes and other items were pushed into the crawl space, but they didn't take up very much room. Beyond them was where I believed "The Order" now lived quietly. I had told them they'd be safe and not bothered back there; far away from the attic's new occupants.

Apparently, they were fine with that.

MY NATIVE AMERICAN VISITOR

I once lived halfway up Oregon's Mount Hood, in a place the local Native Americans had named Brightwood. It featured an old-growth forest with a heavy, dense canopy. The natives liked to gather there during the nicest part of the year, perhaps because it was alive with spirits that inhabited the woods. It was a native tradition to plant give-away keepsake objects in the ground, to give something back to the Earth. This practice seemed to make these grounds even more spirit-filled and enchanted. Many local children had curious stories to tell about things they'd heard in the trees or near a small stream that ran through the place.

The children and the natives weren't the only ones who felt the spirits of Brightwood. An elderly neighbor of mine wrote children's stories under the pen name Omar, because that was the name of the deceased tree that dictated his stories to him. At least that's what he told me as we sat one afternoon on a log from the long-fallen tree.

On a different occasion I thought I heard music along the river, and I followed it through the trees. It sounded like a flute, or even pan-pipes. If I concentrated on it and really tuned my consciousness into it, the music would grow louder. If my concentration waned, the music would grow dim. I don't believe it was physical audio sound but rather a sound I perceived innately, without the use of my ears.

My most amazing and upfront encounter with a spirit in Brightwood happened right in my own home one night around dusk. I saw a spirit appear directly in front of me and then vanish into thin air.

I lived in a rustic house with lots of floor-length windows and a loft bedroom located directly above the living room. Here's how it hap-pened: I was standing at the top of the stairs just inside the doorway to my bedroom. I was about to go downstairs when all of a sudden, a tall Native American in ancient ceremonial dress appeared directly in front of me. He didn't seem wary of me, but just looked around as though disoriented. I think he was surprised to be inside my home. Maybe he was returning to the Brightwood of his ancestors, and my relatively new house just happened to be located on the old ancestral grounds. Or maybe he had never left the place but roamed there constantly as a deceased person in a ghostly life.

In any event, I felt as if we were both inhabiting the same space but were on different planes of existence.

He was muscular and stunning. He wore red and sported a couple of feathers in his long hair. His gaze raced across the room before it met mine, and when it did, he seemed shocked to see me but held his ground. It was almost as if he was waiting for me to respond to him before reacting himself. Honestly, I don't believe he expected to find me there.

I locked my gaze on him and shouted: "Be gone! This is not your house! Be gone now!"

And I waved a hand to one side, as though signaling him to move along. Instantly, he vanished in front of me. My response to him had been a knee-jerk reaction to his sudden presence in my home. I never saw him again, and I never spoke with anyone in Brightwood who admitted to having seen him either.

A RITUAL WALK FROM THE BARN

The community newspaper that I was employed by was located in a building at the bottom of Mount Hood, in an area that was full of old farms from days gone by. This was, after all, Oregon Trail country, and one of the primary branches of the trail ran right through this region. The old Barlow Trail had been used by settlers migrating west, and some of them, having reached the bottom of our mountain, decided they had traveled far enough. The land was fertile here, and on it they built modest pioneer farms.

This had all happened back in the 1800s, and yet I would

occasionally see some of these Oregon pioneers from my car when driving along a certain stretch of road in that area. An old barn door would suddenly open and pioneer men and women dressed in black would start marching out of the barn and across the fields. They carried tools over their shoulders, but I wasn't able to discern whether they were rakes, shovels, pitchforks, or hoes. I could, however, see that these tools had old wooden shafts, which appeared to be quite rough; no doubt the tools were handcrafted.

As I watched, these pioneer figures would perform a task over and over again, as though stuck in some sort of recurring ritual or time loop.

When this occurred I would be headed west at the bottom of the mountain and would see the ghostly apparitions from the corner of my eye.

I would watch them for a few seconds before blinking in astonishment, at which point they'd disappear, and I'd be left to wonder whether I had really seen them at all! But I'd watched them move as a group in a procession—clearly and in great detail. I saw them twice, both times at dusk, and both times I saw exactly the same scene.

I mentioned this to an old resident, herself the descendant of Oregon pioneers.

"Oh, yes," she said. "Yes, I have seen them too."

Then she asked whether I had told anyone else what I'd seen. When I said I hadn't, she said that was probably best.

THE WOMAN IN THE APARTMENT BELOW

After I got married in 1967, my wife and I lived in various apartments in Seattle. One of the best bargains in terms of space—at least at first glance—was a huge triplex on Beacon Hill overlooking Seattle's waterfront. My wife and I were delighted at the low rental price of the apartment, which included the entire second floor of the building. This apartment had a huge living room, a spacious kitchen, and an anteroom with a separate entrance—in addition to the master bedroom and bath. The owner, an architect with a downtown office, may have foreseen the value of this parcel of real estate and a future that included the building of a huge new apartment building on that site, one he may have wished to design and build himself. The top floor of the building (which contained the smallest rental unit), was occupied by a young, single Asian woman.

As prospective tenants my wife and I viewed the apartment one night, accompanied by a woman whose job it was to show us around. When we arrived we found her working on the second floor in the near dark; the rooms were still missing some lightbulbs. The woman seemed a bit despondent and remote as she walked us from room to room, explaining the work that remained for her to do in each one. She also mentioned that the building had a full basement with plenty of storage space for tenants.

Her expression was deadpan and her voice was flat, without much expression or enthusiasm. Clearly she was an unhappy person. I noticed that she wore a wedding ring, but I had been told by the building's owner that she was a single mother with two small children. She and her kids lived in the first-floor apartment, and she was helping the owner by attending to odd jobs around the place.

Touring the large apartment in the dark didn't allow my wife and me to detect the waves of cockroaches that infiltrated the kitchen at night or the mice that inhabited the bedroom. Seeing only what we were allowed to see and loving the view of the Seattle waterfront from the kitchen window, which led to flat-roof sunbathing, we latched on to the Beacon Hill apartment. We had no idea that the house would be haunted—nor did the woman who showed us the place.

When the first of the month rolled around, we started moving our things into the new apartment. We parked our blue rag-top Ghia in front of the big house, but before we could start carrying lamps and clothes up its winding staircase, we noticed a lot of commotion out front and inside the first-floor apartment. The first thing that caught our attention was a fire department medical aid truck and emergency technicians wheeling a gurney out the front door. There was a cover draped over the gurney. When the EMTs descended the front steps to the curb, an arm fell out from under the sheet. I recognized the ring on the hand of the lifeless body as belonging to the woman who had showed us the apartment just a few days earlier. Blood trickled from the hand that pointed down to the ground.

The EMTs brushed hurriedly by us. As we walked up to the building we passed the doorway of the first-floor apartment and saw the woman's two children watching cartoons on a TV in the living room. The kids held plates of spaghetti in their hands, which were messy with red tomato sauce, and they sat laughing on the floor. Apparently they weren't fully aware of what had just happened to their mother. At the other end of the living room the door to the bathroom was wide open. We could see blood on the sink and all over the floor.

The children continued to watch cartoons and laugh at them, oblivious to the tragedy. The red tomato sauce on their plates provided a stark counterpoint to the red blood in the bathroom.

The kids were gone by the time we'd finished moving in, and the first-floor apartment was vacant and silent.

In a few days, however, we began to notice sounds in the apartment below. We couldn't place them at first, but then determined that they seemed to be footsteps. The house was old and its floorboards squeaked underfoot. The footsteps sounded like pacing, and the pacing always seemed to take place in the middle of the night. It sounded as if someone was walking nervously, restlessly, back and forth.

Since the kitchen roaches and bedroom mice were bigger problems for us, however, my wife and I pretty much ignored the strange sounds on the floor below. We figured they were none of our business and probably just our imagination anyway, even though we both heard the strange sounds at the same time every night.

Eventually I decided to install a darkroom in the basement. There I could process film, a hobby I'd picked up through my newspaper work. I wasn't intent on constructing anything elaborate—as long as it was dark and had running water it would do. The old basement seemed perfect for this, because there were no windows in the back. In fact, a small room had been built into the far corner of the basement, and it seemed absolutely pitch black back there. To make sure no light would possibly slip through the cracks, however, I wrapped black plastic around the door frame, and around the wall that faced out to the basement's entry and windows.

The darkroom contained a workbench but no tools. There were old stand-up radios from the golden days of early radio elsewhere in the basement, so I figured that the workbench and shop enclosure might have been where somebody had once restored old radios.

The only time I had to play in my darkroom was in the evening, after work, which I saw as a huge plus because the late hour of the day would no doubt make the darkroom even darker. But there was a problem. Whenever I set up my developing trays and darkroom timer on the workbench, a strange light would appear. It was impossible for me to determine where the light originated or the nature of it. It just seemed to come out of nowhere and cast itself across the workbench.

It was eerie and gave me shivers. After a couple of attempts to use the makeshift darkroom, I gave up because this light precluded me from developing my film. At first I didn't mention this strange situation to anyone. It baffled me, and I felt a bit silly that I couldn't resolve it on my own.

I went down to the basement again a few days later to deconstruct the darkroom and put my things away. When I was done, I emerged from the darkroom to discover a young man moving the big, old radios around. He was working as fast as he could, wrestling the tall radio casings up the basement stairs. When he saw me watching him, he explained that he had been a tenant in the building but had recently moved out, leaving his radios behind. "Yeah, I spent a lot of time down here, working on these old radios," he told me. "My wife sort of resented all the time I spent on them."

"You lived on the first floor?" I asked.

He nodded.

"And you have two kids?" I continued.

"Yeah," he said. "My wife and I were separated. Then she died. The kids are now living with me."

Suddenly it all made sense. It was his wife who was haunting the house; a restless spirit who had committed suicide.

Actually, this didn't frighten me, nor—when I told my wife—did it seem to frighten her. This woman was a sad spirit who had clearly found no peace in death but was harmless. I doubt if she was even aware of our presence. She was preoccupied with her own past and her determination to remain in that house.

We lived in that apartment without concern for some time, enjoying the harbor view. The last time I drove by the house, years later, curtains were blowing out of one of its windows and the place looked almost deserted, to say nothing of haunted.

MY MOTHER'S DEAD BROTHER

My mother liked to tell a story about her brother, which shaped my opinion that ghosts are friendly, confused souls who merely had a little occasional trouble crossing over to the other side. Spirits don't seem bound by the physical laws of the universe as the living are. Instead, they seem capable of moving freely through time, as this tale will illustrate.

My mother was close to her older brother, who had joined the Navy and, as a young man, left the family farm. He worked as a medic in the Philippines, and unfortunately when he came home after World War II he had tuberculosis, which was not detected immediately. Vern visited my mother and our family after his military service was completed, and he and my mother reminisced about their early days on the farm. At one point he told her how much he wanted to return to the farm to see it again.

He died shortly after visiting us, fresh out of the service. It was a sudden death that seemed to catch everyone by surprise. Did Vern ever get to return to the farm one last time? And if so, would it be just as he had remembered it?

My mother would tell this story in two parts, actually. The events of the first part happened one hot summer day—when she was a girl back on the farm. There she saw a young man in a white dress shirt who looked out of place. He was walking across the pen in back of the family house, toward a gate. He didn't seem to notice anyone around him, even though my mother waved at him. She thought she recognized him in a way. He looked like her older brother Vern, but he appeared to be years older than Vern, who would have been only ten at that time. The man's face was similar, however, as was his wavy black hair. He even whistled the same way her brother whistled. But when he opened the gate and walked through it, he seemed to vanish in front of her eyes. She never saw him there again.

The second part of my mother's story takes place years later, after Vern had died. When she was mourning his death and reminiscing about him, she remembered the mysterious visitor she'd seen years earlier at the family farm. She decided that the man she'd seen looked just like her brother the way he looked when he died.

Maybe my uncle had found a way to visit his family farm one more time to see it just the way it had looked to him as a boy. I assume he dropped by that one last time and then left the place forever.

I'd like to think that his eternal spirit has moved on and found peace.

SPIRIT COMMUNICATION

Ghosts are sometimes known to communicate with the living through electronic devices like the telephone. I have a personal story to tell about a ghost who reached out from the dead across phone lines.

My brother died suddenly in North Dakota, far from his nuclear family. His relationship with my sister, who lived miles away in Washington state, had been a difficult one. I lived many miles east of him at the time of his passing. Because of these distances between us, my sister and I decided to have him cremated immediately and bury his ashes later.

On the day of his cremation, my sister received a frantic call from someone who screamed at her and claimed he was burning up. It sounded exactly like our dead brother. What made the identification even easier for my sister were the names he called her—names that he'd called her as a child. Other family members heard him on the phone that day, and they all agreed that the voice they heard sounded exactly like our brother's voice.

I too got mysterious phone calls when I worked at Quest Books in Wheaton, Illinois. My office in the southern corner of the second floor of the Theosophical Publishing House was above a bookstore and shipping area on the floor below. It had once been a residential apartment. One summer, on a very regular basis, I started to receive phone calls from a man with a thick East Indian accent. He was very polite in inviting me to join him on what he called "lightning tours" of India in August, which he told me he had been leading for many years. He never left his name or number but said that he'd call me back for my answer.

I started to think that this must be some sort of an office prank, and I pressed people in our operation to see if they had called me and faked the exquisite East Indian accent of an old man. By their confused expressions, I concluded that they knew nothing about it. The next time the old man called me, I told him I would be unable to join him on his lightning tour of India that August. He suggested that I keep it in mind for another year, since it would be ideal for me, and it would change my life forever. He then offered me some unsolicited personal advice on meditation. He told me always to meditate in the early-morning light beside a body of water.

After that, many days passed without a phone call from him, and I began to wonder who he was. Could he be somebody famous? He had seemed so knowledgeable. I wandered downstairs to our bookstore and scanned the books by Indian authors who wrote about meditation. On the back of one such book I read the description of a renowned teacher who had delighted in organizing lightning tours to India every August. The author advocated meditating outside by a body of water in the early-morning light. The author had been dead for quite some time.

2
Meeting My Ghost-Hunting Teacher

One summer I met a woman who taught me how to make contact with spirits who haunted houses or grounds and how to convince them to leave. It all sounded easy enough. She walked me slowly through the fundamentals of what I might expect to find and instructed me as to various techniques to employ in order to get them to leave if they proved unwilling to go. She'd been successful in this line of work so I figured that I could just follow her step-by-step procedure.

The place where I met Helen was Orcas Island in the magical San Juan Islands between Seattle and Vancouver. There are approximately 172 islands in the chain. Orcas Island, an island shaped like a horseshoe, is one of the largest and most mystical of them.

Many factors drew me to Orcas Island initially, one of which was a wonderful retreat center called Indralaya. The island also was home to a publishing and marketing alliance group called NAPRA; I was on its original board of directors. A lovely state park and resort graced the island, causing me to fantasize about moving there with a big sailboat, for sailboats were everywhere in its waters. In addition, a mineral hot springs bubbled up on the island's far side. Orcas

Island also featured a beautiful mountain, at the top of which deer and other woodsy creatures roamed freely. And then there was the enchanted Outlook Inn in the village of Eastsound, where most of the island's tiny population resided.

The newspaper where I worked in Anacortes, Washington, sent me to Orcas Island once a year to research stories for the summer magazine that the paper published. While there, I typically stayed at the Outlook Inn, which had been built by the mystical author Louis Gittner, a gifted psychic who went into deep trances much like those of Edgar Cayce. My understanding is that Louis's mother had served for a time as a secretary to the great Cayce. When she left his employ, the sleeping prophet had foretold great things for her son, all of which came to pass.

Lying on his back in a darkened room in which the shades had been drawn, Louis would enter into a trance state. Even though the room was dark, lights would frequently descend from nowhere to dance across his chest. Louis would then speak in a voice different from his own and provide insights that seemed to be channeled through him. He was the subject of a phenomenal book called *Words from the Source* and the author of several others, including *There Is a Rainbow, Love Is a Verb,* and *Listen, Listen, Listen*—all of which were in my personal library and some of which had been signed by him. These books had helped me transform my life.

Louis was a big man with a large smile and childlike enthusiasm. It was impossible not to feel absolutely safe, relaxed, and comfortable in his company, even if you didn't really know him all that well. I had met him only a handful of times on my trips to the island over the years. So in a sense, although I had known him for many years, I hadn't actually spent all that much time with him.

He was gifted and self-deprecating and didn't like to call attention to himself and his talents. If people who passed through the island stopped at his inn and happened to "discover" him on their own, then he would engage with them; his students just seemed to find him.

Louis had once read my energy field and told me that I was sensitive. He also told me secrets about the grounds of the inn and the log chapel that he had built behind it. He told me how to see the energy spirits who inhabited the grounds and spoke through him.

One summer I arrived at the island with some friends from work who I wanted to introduce to Louis. I asked for him at the front desk, and then my friends and I waited for him in the dining room. I expected him to come out and chat with me as he usually did.

Instead, a dark-haired woman approached our table and introduced herself. "I'm Helen, Louis's secretary," she told us. "Louis can't meet with you at the moment, so he asked me to do so instead." She told me that she had been with Louis for some time now and assisted him with various matters around the inn. We made small talk for a few moments, and then I asked her what her background was.

At that point she volunteered the following information: "I de-ghost houses," she told me.

No doubt I looked intrigued, for she then asked me, "Is that something that interests you?"

I nodded as she continued talking without pause. "Because if it does interest you, I can tell you how I do it and what you're likely to encounter in this sort of work. It's pretty interesting, really. It's always amazing what you find, although perhaps it's not what you might expect.

Helen had a lot of experience communicating with ghosts, and she went on to tell us some stories about these experiences, which appeared to scare my two traveling companions a bit, although they would never admit to that. Me, I just drank it all in; I couldn't get enough of it.

Yes, Helen was very insightful and very sensitive. She could just walk into a house and immediately spot the ghost hiding in the room. "A lot of the time," she said, "what you'll find is a little old lady sitting in a corner with her coat and hat on and maybe holding a purse. She's waiting to go somewhere, but she just doesn't leave. Maybe she doesn't exactly realize that she's died. Or maybe she doesn't *want* to move on. Or perhaps she's just unsure *how* to move on."

"What do you do in that case?" I asked Helen.

"Oh, you just sit quietly with her for a while and sort of hold her hand. You try to make her feel comfortable and supported. You tell her that you understand how she feels. Then you begin to encourage her to move on."

I had never had such a conversation with a ghost, and so I asked Helen, "What if they really don't know how to move on?"

"Really, everyone who dies knows instinctively how to move on," she told me. "But they're just hesitant or don't trust their instincts."

"So you don't have to lead them out of the premises they're haunting?" I asked her.

"Not normally. You just talk with them, reassure them, and then back away. They'll just disappear on their own. It's pretty natural."

I wondered if Helen was telling me the whole story.

"Is it generally that easy?" I asked hopefully.

"Well, not always . . ." she admitted.

I asked her if she ever came across spirits who proved to be difficult by refusing to leave.

"Well, then you have a *real* haunting," was her answer. "But there are *always* ways to get them to go."

Helen stood up and said she'd get us some coffee, and when we demurred she insisted. I watched her pull away from the table with a tight smile. When she returned, she seemed preoccupied for a few moments as she passed the cream and sugar around. Then she turned to me, her gaze softening.

"A lot of times," she said, "what you actually find when you get a report of a haunted house or a haunted building is not really a ghost at all."

I gave her a very puzzled looked. She paused to carefully phrase her explanation.

"Look," she said, "ghosts are just one of the spirits you might encounter when you walk into one of these houses. Oh, the people will tell you the place is haunted with ghosts all right, but that's not always the case."

I just shook my head; I wasn't following her at all.

"Okay," Helen said. "Let's say I get a call to go into somebody's house because they're hearing strange noises or because they see something abnormal lurking around. Or maybe the people are feeling some sort of strange eerie chill when they go into a certain room. They're thinking ghosts.

"But when I get there, maybe what I'll really see is some dark brooding hulk that's like a cloud of dark energy. It might take the form of a person, but it's not anyone's dead relative. It's an energy mass that people put there."

Helen looked at me closely to see if any of this was resonating with me.

"You see, a lot of dark energies that seem to haunt houses are totally created by the people who live there. When they argue and fight, their negative energy forms something that begins to take shape and occupy the house they live in. And when they continue to feed it with their negative emotions, this emotional energy gives it even more of a defined shape. These emotions can be rage, hatred, or frustration, or any other dark emotion that's potentially hurtful and destructive. In time, this dark energy begins to look a lot like a person. And that's nothing you want in your house," she added.

I asked her how a person might get rid of such a dark phantom.

"It's not easy," she told me. "Just finding it and confronting it doesn't do much. Unless the people who created it alter their behavior, they'll just continue to sustain it and strengthen it, and it won't leave. The people who created it need to dissolve it. Without emotional energy to feed it, it'll eventually die. Now that's not an easy thing to tell people who want you to walk into their home and chase away some ghost for them."

The concept of people forming their own demons out of their negative thoughtforms shocked me, and I quizzed Helen about this. I figured that I must have misunderstood her or read something more into what she'd said. When she assured me that everyone has the ability to change things for the better or for the worse and form energy from their thoughtforms, I expressed my utter amazement.

She just smiled.

I had a hard time accepting that anything that seemed as private and shapeless as our thoughts could be directed in such a way. She assured me that it happened a lot, but most people are completely oblivious to the possibility of this. They fail to acknowledge the power of consciousness as pure energy in motion.

"So our demons are man-made?" I asked her.

"Yes, I suppose that's one way to say it," she said. She went over it all again for me. "In this case, that would certainly be true. Absolutely. It comes down to how you choose to direct your emotional energy. What I'm talking about is the worst case, one in which people lose control of their emotional energy, and they have an emotional outburst, filled with anger and all sorts of powerful, negative thoughts. These thoughts take aim like arrows, and they stick where they're directed.

"People don't even realize that they're doing this. Sometimes you get a whole houseful of people doing this. There's no place for the negative energy to go but into some corner of the house where it gets bundled up into something hideous and monstrous. Then the people who live there call me, because they think they heard something and figure their house is haunted by a ghost. But they, the people who live there, are really the source of the problem."

Helen paused for a moment to pour everyone a glass of water from a pitcher on the table. She probably figured we needed a little cooling down after that revelation.

"Is that—uh—is that common in terms of what you might find in a haunting, in your experience?" I finally asked her.

She took a swallow of water before venturing an answer.

"Common, no—but it does happen," she said. "And it may be more common than we'd like to imagine. Most of the time our negative thoughts don't get all balled up like that. It's more like they become a dust bunny in the corner, or a small cloud that floats around the room."

"That's good, "I said. "You really had me scared for a minute there!"

She laughed as she pushed a strand of dark hair out of her face. "Most of the time de-ghosting houses is pretty simple," she said.

"And you can just see these ghosts and walk up to talk with them?" I asked her.

"Yes, it's often just that easy," Helen assured me. "Although they might be surprised that somebody can detect them. They may have been in the same spot for a long time and don't feel any particular attachment to anyone living in the house. They might not even notice the people walking around them very much. They are pretty out of it, in a sense."

I wanted to know how she opened up meaningful communication with them.

"You don't speak aloud in a normal fashion," she replied. "You sort of tune in to their thoughts. You have to tune in to them to feel them. Then you can sense their thoughts—their feelings and concerns mostly. And they can read you the same way."

"Telepathy?" I asked her.

"Yes," she responded, "thoughts, not words."

I asked her whether the ghosts were ever wary of her and if they tried to run away.

"Where would they run?" she answered. "They're so lost to begin with. They don't know where to go or what to do. Once you lock in to them, you have them."

"Have them?"

"Well, I just mean that you have their attention. Oh, I guess they could become frightened of you, but I don't find that to be the case very often. You just go slow and assure them that you want to help them—that you're not any threat."

That sounded simple enough to me.

"So do you want to try de-ghosting houses?" Helen asked me.

I looked at my two friends who were gripping their water glasses tightly. They just smiled and gave me weak looks with a kind of turned-off expression that seemed to say, "I don't know about this sort of thing." I looked back at Helen. She was calm and collected, as though what she was talking about was no big deal at all.

"Yeah," I said. "I could do this. I've seen ghosts before. I could probably help. But you'll have to teach me the tricks."

"There's really not a whole lot to it, as I've said," Helen responded. "I could walk you through a few common approaches for salting a building, staking haunted grounds—little things like that. Mostly you don't need to worry about doing anything more, but sometime you might come upon a haunting, an old haunting somewhere, that might be harder to deal with."

I wanted to learn more but my friends were getting restless, so I told Helen that we'd be on the island until the next night and could meet with her again the following day, if that would be convenient for her.

She nodded.

"Just ask for me at the front desk. I'll be here all day tomorrow. Late mornings are usually best."

I thanked her and started to pull a few bills out of my wallet to pay for the coffee but she just waved it off.

"Louis set up this meeting. Don't worry about it. Have a nice evening."

I told her that we were going to the mineral hot springs at the other end of the island. She put one hand on my shoulder in a friendly way before she stood up to leave.

After she left the dining room and disappeared into the offices at the back of the inn, I sat with my friends, a bit dumbfounded.

What a remarkable woman, I thought to myself. How selfless and brave.

After our meeting with Helen, my friends and I rode in silence to Doe Bay Village, which had been the grounds of an artists' colony in the 1930s. The old cabins at Doe Bay now provided lodging to tourists who were drawn to the nearby mineral hot springs. The springs emerged from a tiny creek on the side of the road in front of Doe Bay Village and could easily be overlooked, given that they looked more like a little ditch overgrown with weeds. The people who ran Doe Bay in those days were more into yoga than aesthetics. They built enclosures, put up tents, and remodeled the cabins. They also rented out kayaks and ran a small café on the grounds.

What drew us to the village were the mineral baths—one hot and one cold. The cold mineral spring water was piped into a huge tub and heated. Next to that hot tub, an adjacent tub of similar size was filled with natural cold spring water. People would soak in the hot tub and then take a fast dip in the cold tub. And many people soaked naked, given that clothing was optional. Nearby, a cedar-lined sauna gave people a place to wrap up in towels and warm up after their immersion in the mineral bath. You could sit in the sauna and slowly sweat off toxins from every pore of your body before going for a healthy dip in the mineral hot tubs outside.

My buddies and I soaked in the hot mineral bath for a good long time without saying too much. We were a little stunned by Helen's ghost stories. We had never met anyone who went looking for ghosts and then just walked up to them and started talking to them—if "talking" is the right word.

We finished with a cold dip, skipped the sauna, and then dressed pretty much in silence. The interlude had been relaxing, and it helped us to unwind after Helen's stirring tales, which had left me with a lot of questions.

I wouldn't be able to talk to her again until the following day. In the meantime, I wanted some insights on the matter from Louis, whose psychic gifts and wisdom I greatly admired.

Perhaps we would encounter him that evening at the inn.

The five-minute ride back to the village of Eastsound put us in front of the Outlook Inn at just about dinnertime. In that part of the world in the summer, sunlight lasts late into the day, given that the sun doesn't begin to set on the San Juan Islands until after 9:00 p.m.

We parked directly in front of the inn, just off the main street that runs through the village and across the island. A waiter brought us to our choice of tables. My friends seemed to favor the same table by the roadside window where we had sat earlier in the day with Helen. Maybe they just wanted to keep an eye on the car. Or maybe they wanted to watch the sailboats in the bay as the sun began to set, leaving ripples of glittering water as it retreated. The magic of the sun setting and the moon rising over the island made for a beautiful evening on the waterfront.

After we were seated, I asked our server if Louis was available to come out for a minute to say hello. This was not always as likely as it had been during previous years when I would visit him at the inn because the passage of time and ill health had taken its toll on him. His deep sleeping trances, wherein he surrendered his body to the ordeal of channeling words from something that his biographer Brad Steiger called "the Source," generally left him extremely hungry and tired.

Louis himself seemed to have no clue as to the source of the information he received in his trances. In one session, however, speaking through Louis, "the Source" had identified itself as a collection of energies. Louis found parallels between the energies that spoke through him and the nature spirits and devas who channeled information to members of the famous spiritual center of Findhorn in Scotland. In fact, Louis had once taken his personal daily journal to Findhorn to compare transmissions he'd received on a specific date, at a specific time. Amazingly, he found them to be virtually identical to messages received at Findhorn at exactly the same time.

Louis had designed the inn, decorated its rooms, and planned the meals served in the dining room. He was as good a chef as he was a writer and a psychic. As a result, the restaurant, as well as the inn, was always packed with guests. I can attest that the food was first-rate. I always consumed too much during my meals there and ordered just about anything and everything that would fit on my table.

We told our server that we'd place our order after chatting with Louis, if he could be found. We sat drinking coffee, hoping to see the psychic of Orcas Island. Busy as he must have been on this night at the height of the summer tourist season, he soon joined us. Many diners waved or smiled appreciatively to him as he passed through the dining room.

When he approached our table I told him that we had had a nice conversation with Helen that day and we were very appreciative of the time she'd spent with us. Then I motioned for him to join us. After I introduced him to my friends, he pulled up a chair and sat down.

There were so many questions I wanted to ask him, but I tried to focus on just a few of the more pressing ones. I began by telling him how appreciative I was of the fact that he brought forth sound information of an upbeat nature whenever the collection of energies who gathered around him spoke through him.

"Yes, I am very fortunate, I think," he told me. "Not everyone is as fortunate."

I mentioned how trance mediums often brought suspect messages across the veil and that more recent channelers were often criticized as much for the message and source of their message as for their approach.

"Really, when I'm in a trance state, it's like being in a crowded rail-way station," Louis said. "It's filled with many voices and many agen-das. It's confusing, with everyone speaking at once and trying to come forward. I don't recommend trying it."

"Because it's confusing or because it's dangerous?" I asked.

"Both," he replied. "Everywhere you turn, spirits are talking at you and pulling at you, trying to get your attention."

"What do they want?" I asked him.

"They want to come home with you. And you don't know the good ones from the bad ones, because you've just arrived and you're disori-ented yourself."

I asked him when it got easier.

"It gets easier with experience. At this point I know which spirits I can trust and want to listen to, and which ones to avoid. But I've been doing this for some time. And the ones who visit me have an ongoing rapport with me; we have an established relationship, which minimizes the risk."

I wanted to know how he could sense which ones to trust. I also wanted to know how I could trust a spirit I might encounter when entering a haunted house with the intent of clearing it of its ghosts, as Helen did. I didn't want to undercut his secretary, however, by talking about her work behind her back.

"Think of the place we go to in the trance state as a crossroads," Louis continued. "Most of the spirits who reach this crossroads are taken aback when they get there and uncertain where to go or what to do. And spirits are piling in all the time, coming from everywhere," he reiterated. "That's why I liken it to a crossroads, or a train station, you see. Spirits are railroaded there and then find themselves off the track in an unfamiliar place."

"Soul voyagers?" I said. "Astral travelers lost in their astral travels?"

"Yes, they're a bit lost in their travels in this great adventure of the spirit. Mind you, these aren't people—they're spirit entities. Many of them are hoping for a ride back on your train. They want to come into your world, your life, your home."

He looked at me closely to see if I was beginning to grasp it.

"A lot of these spirit entities," he continued, "shouldn't be trusted. They're dark spirits, not interested in the human condition or helping us in any way. They have their own business, their own agenda."

I closed my eyes.

"As I said, with time, it becomes easier to sort all this out," Louis told me. "It's just very confusing at first, and you have to be careful. You don't want to bring a lot of things from out there back into your world. That's all."

"That's a *lot.*"

He laughed the laugh of a gifted psychic who had traveled beyond this world many times over and always found his way back safely, rewarded with insights from a higher plane. I, on the other hand, wasn't sure how to get safely out of the room.

I had so much to learn!

Louis reminded me of the log cabin in the back of his inn and how, on one occasion, he had directed me to sit in it at midnight, in the dark. He told me that in doing this, I would be able to see the energy spirits that spoke to him and surrounded his bountiful gardens.

That had been on a previous outing, and I remembered the occasion well. Little flecks of light, one at a time, had entered the log cabin's chapel from the front of the building, slipping between the logs Louis had brought to the island to build the cabin with. The lights, which to my untrained eye resembled fireflies, zoomed and darted through the building and past me, my son, and a lady friend who was with us. After racing through the chapel, these strange flecks of light exited through slight gaps in the logs at the rear of the building.

"Those energy spirits were amazing and wonderful!" I recounted to Louis. "They were totally benevolent. And the best part of all is that I had two reliable witnesses with me when I made contact with them!"

Louis just smiled.

"And what did you ask the energy spirits?" he asked me.

"Ask them?" I repeated. "I didn't think to ask them anything. Oh, gosh. What a missed opportunity, right?"

He put a hand on my shoulder, as if to say there would be other chances. I could see that he was getting restless and was ready to end our chat.

I flashed back to Helen and her "de-ghosting" of houses, as she put it. Maybe that was more my speed—just chatting up deceased people who needed a bit of friendly assurance to move on spiritually, leaving this world behind. Helen's sort of work didn't seem to bring dangerous spirits into the world, but ushered spirits out of this one—a noble bit of housekeeping, I thought.

Yes, I would meet with Helen the following day and find out more about her work. How hard could it be?

3
Helen's Ghost-Hunting Instructions

Despite the fact that I liked Helen, her stories scared me a bit. Going into haunted houses at the invitation of people who were unhappy with otherworldly guests who refused to leave couldn't be as easy as she made it sound. Running down ghosts and then convincing them to hit the road sounded tough to me, no matter how much she sugar-coated it.

But perhaps it was easy for *her*. Psychic readings were easy for Louis. Both of them stayed in a safe zone and hadn't had many bad experiences. Maybe they were charmed or special somehow. The spirits they found all seemed to be reasonably tame and easy to handle.

If I trained under someone like that, then how could anything go wrong for me? I kept running that bit of logic through my head as we left the inn for our stroll by the bay after dinner. It was cool at that hour, and the sunset over the water was incredibly beautiful. The moon looked immense in the endlessly starry sky, and moonlight danced upon the waves that drifted ashore on the incoming tide. We walked down to a small waterfront park across the road from the inn. The park extended halfway through the village and followed the curvy road that ran through Eastsound. Although the night was beautiful, we quickly discovered that the bugs were also enjoying the warm summer evening, so we left the beach to them and headed back to our lodgings.

The stairs to the left of the dining room led to a large hallway and the guest rooms of the inn. The room I shared with my friends was quite large, with multiple beds, a small writing desk, and old-style wallpaper. It had been tastefully appointed with period pieces, resembling a room from the Victorian age, and it made me feel as though I was living in another century. My thoughts returned to the subject of ghost hunting. Our room appeared old; might it be haunted? The answer was no, for although the room had been made to look antiquated, the building itself was quite new. Everybody who had ever stayed in this room, on this floor, or in this large building by the bay had undoubtedly been happy during their time here, and most likely no one had ever died on the premises, I reasoned.

My friends were ready for sleep and had already dimmed the lights and turned down their beds. There was no television (indeed, who watched TV in the Victorian era?). So I went to bed and tried to sleep as well, but I just couldn't seem to drift off. There was too much on my mind, with all the talk of ghosts and spirits floating somewhere out there, waiting for someone or something to haunt. I took off my shoes and pulled a straight-backed wooden chair up to the small writing desk.

Time to make some notes, I figured.

Being a journalist, I decided to outline my upcoming talk with Helen. I'd discovered that if I thought an upcoming interview might be difficult or awkward, it was extremely helpful to write out my list of questions beforehand. I had lots of questions for Helen, and it was unlikely that I'd be returning to the island anytime soon. Besides, she might not even be here on my next trip. After all, I hadn't seen her on my earlier visits—but perhaps that was because she'd been out de-ghosting houses at the time.

I looked over to Fred and Ian, who were falling asleep. I had dragged them with me to this island, telling them how many fun things there were to do in the San Juan Islands in the summertime. But all we had done was visit with Helen and Louis and make a trip to the mineral springs. And for all I knew, Helen's discourse might have sounded like a crazy bit of fabrication to them. Ah well, they'd soon be back at work at the paper and their time on the island would no doubt be pretty much forgotten.

I was on a different track. Intrigued by the little I'd learned about ghost hunting, I was now determined to get the whole story. So I pulled out some of that writing paper that one typically finds in hotel guest rooms: those half-sheets of stationery with the name of the inn at the top. I also found a pen in the drawer. I proceeded to write up my first set of notes, which would soon become an outline on how to de-ghost houses. As usual, my reporter's notations were sketchy with lots of abbreviations. I would bring the outline, such as it was, with me the following day for my meeting with Helen.

My questions for her were as follows:

1. How long have you been de-ghosting houses?
2. How were you trained?
3. Do you always work alone?
4. How do you prepare or set up?
5. Do you use tools and, if so, what are they?
6. How long does the entire de-ghosting process take?
7. What do you tell people in the house when you de-ghost their house for them?
8. Do you have everyone leave the premises when you are working there?
9. Would you describe some of your toughest cases?
10. Do you charge for your services?
11. Are there ever any reprisals or repercussions from this kind of work?
12. Does this kind of work ever take its toll on you?

I stopped at an even dozen conversation starters. These questions should give us plenty to discuss. And my questions—if they were the right ones—would no doubt lead to others. Besides, this wasn't a newspaper interview—it wasn't for publication. It was just for me. I folded the little half-slip of stationery paper and stuffed it into my wallet in preparation for the following day.

The next morning after a light island breakfast of yogurt, berries, and other fruit, my friends and I sat in the dining room, waiting for Helen. No doubt she was pretty busy at this time of day, given her professional position as secretary for the Louis Foundation, Mr. Gittner's publishing company. Her duties must have been numerous and probably extended far beyond the obvious tasks of helping to run the Outlook Inn. I idly wondered if she handled all of the correspondence for the inn, the foundation, and for Louis in his role as author. A secretary is typically an expert multi-tasker, and I doubted that Helen was an exception to this rule.

When our waiter appeared I inquired as to Helen's availability once more. He assured us that she knew we were there and waiting to see her whenever she had a few free moments. So we waited patiently, drinking coffee as we did so. My friend Ian began to read a Seattle daily newspaper he had found on the front counter. He was turning to the sports page, presumably to see whether the Mariners had had the right stuff the previous night. Fred just drank from his fancy coffee cup and watched the bedraggled tourists who littered the otherwise elegant Victorian room. The tourists were all decked out in shades, sandals, shorts, halter tops, and straw hats—beachcombers all.

I was about to visit the rest room when Helen rushed in. She waved and smiled, as though to indicate that things had been a bit hectic and she was sorry she'd kept us waiting. She pulled up a chair from a vacant table nearby and sat, sort of prim and proper, on the edge of it.

"Sorry!" she announced. "Never know what's waiting for me in the morning!"

I told her that we had had a nice chat with Louis the previous evening wherein he had told us a thing or two about spirits, although he wasn't talking about ghosts specifically. Reaching for my wallet, I pulled out my piece of paper with its questions for Helen on it.

"My, you even have notes!" Helen commented as her gaze fell upon it. I noticed her fingernails, which were neatly trimmed, neither too long nor too fancy. They were unpainted, but clean. These are the hands of someone who isn't afraid of work, I thought to myself.

"If you want to look over a few of these questions I have," I said, "perhaps I'll slip away to the washroom for a minute to give you time to read them."

But she was already reading the paper, or trying to decipher my pen scrawls, I should say. I saw a perplexed look in her eyes as she tried to take in my questions.

I dashed off to the rest room, and on my return I saw that she'd refolded the paper and pushed it to my side of the table.

"Did you read both sides?" I asked her.

"No matter," she said. "Let's just talk for a bit. Then you can ask me any questions you want."

I nodded.

"What's your personal interest in ghosts?" she asked me. "You seemed unusually interested in my stories yesterday."

I told her about all of the ghosts or ghostlike spirits that I'd seen in my life, and we had a good laugh about cats that hang around after they die. Apparently she'd had a cat like that too, and also a little ghost dog. She actually seemed quite impressed with the Native American spirit that had popped into my house one day and the scribbled messages left in my attic by "The Order."

When I got to the part about the sad dead woman in the first-floor apartment in Seattle, the one who wandered aimlessly at night and haunted the basement darkroom, Helen frowned and held up a finger to stop me.

"*Those* are the ones *I* work with," she said proudly.

I told her how depressing it had been for me to hear that woman pacing the floor at night, although she hadn't really frightened my wife and me. "She filled the whole building with sadness," I told Helen. "We had no idea what to do, other than try to block out the sounds and ignore them, if we could."

Helen nodded and seemed genuinely moved.

"Yes, ghosts are ritualistic, it seems. They'll haunt a place in the same way and at the same time of day or night. And they might do it for years and years, until they are freed to move on. Your neighbor from the floor below you might *still* be there, even if the building has been leveled and a new building raised in its place."

I told Helen that I was ready to learn her tricks about how to communicate with ghosts and get them to move on peacefully.

"Okay," she said. "If that's what you really want."

I picked up my list of questions but she waved her hand over the piece of paper as though to say, "Just leave it."

"Most of the time, you'll simply go into a house or a building that's being haunted and try to find the ghost so that you can approach it and connect with it," Helen said. "You might be wondering how you'll know that the house is actually haunted?" she said, anticipating my next question. "The people there will tell you that they hear things, feel things, see things, or sense things. Sometimes they'll be wrong and it'll turn out to be something like a noisy neighbor or just the natural settling of an old house. Often, though, you'll find that a certain room or area of the house will seem cold. Or odd things might happen in one particular room—things that the people who live there can't quite explain.

"When you first get to the house," she continued, "you should listen to what the people who live there have to say about it. Then you tell them that you've heard enough and need to work alone for a while. You sit down and get into a certain space in your head. You put your feelers on. You get into a zone where you tune out a lot of things and really listen psychically. It takes practice, but you can learn to do it. Don't try to talk or think too much when you do this. You need to tune in to the spirit world around you."

I started to make some new notes. She covered the paper, as though to say, "Just listen."

"If you can't tune in to the spirit that people tell you is haunting their house, then the house isn't really haunted or else you can't help them. You've got to tune in to the spirit to be able to communicate with it."

Helen looked me in the eye carefully to see that I was getting it and then sat back and relaxed a little bit, seemingly satisfied.

"When you sense the spirit, maybe you'll feel it before you can see it. Or maybe you'll hear it before you're able to actually see it. Often, you'll sense a kind of tingling feeling. Actually, it's possible to make contact with it without ever actually seeing it. And I need to explain that to you, I think . . .

"Not everyone is clairvoyant," she continued. "Maybe you're more clairaudient than clairvoyant, meaning that you can *hear* things psychically but perhaps not *see* things psychically. Also, clairvoyant seeing is not seeing in exactly the same way that you normally see with your eyes. Remember, we're dealing with the nonphysical realm—the spirit realm that you're approaching from the outside. You see what you see with your mind's eye, and a picture of what's out there forms on a screen inside your head as kind of mental image. Got that?"

I nodded.

"It might take you some time to establish where the ghost is hiding and to sense where it may be lurking in the house. Just take your time. When you feel you're starting to sense it, you might start roaming around until you feel you're getting closer and may be moving in on it. When you feel that the spirit is very close, just stay right where you are until things become a little clearer for you. Hopefully you'll see it, or see it in your mind's eye. Try to get some sense of what it looks like—whether it's a man, woman, or child. Try to see or sense a face. Try to sense its expression and how it feels. Tune in to your ghost.

"They might very likely know that you're doing that, so don't move quickly or make any movements or sounds that might scare them off. Let them become comfortable with you. At that point, the two of you will begin to synch up.

"Hopefully you're now sitting with it or standing near it in a friendly way that's warm and cordial. In the hollow half-world they live in, this could be very comforting to them and may be the only real comfort they've known in a long time. Remember, their lives are unsettled. They wander without peace, all alone. They're lost souls, quite literally."

I asked how to talk with them, given that I couldn't make a sound.

"Speak without words," she said quickly. "Without sound. This isn't the physical world, remember. You're crossing the veil into the spirit world. You'll speak psychically. You'll think thoughts. Forget words. Forget sentences. Form pictures and images in your mind's eye, inside your head. Then send these thoughts to them."

Fred stirred to life with a question. "What do you say to them to get them to go, if you don't mind my asking?"

"You form an image in your head—without words—that suggests there's nothing there for them any longer," Helen said. "You empathize with them and send them love and concern for their well-being. Generally, they can pick up on that and read you. Emotional energy is something they can grasp rather easily.

"Then it's just a matter of being convincing with them," Helen said. "Maybe you'll send them a mental picture of the house's occupants being disturbed by them. Help them to understand that these poor people are the rightful inhabitants of the house now. These new occupants of the house are the living. Life in the physical world is for the living, not the dead.

"Then tell them that they're dead. Perhaps they don't fully realize that, or they're in a state of denial about it. They need to acknowledge the fact that they're dead and realize that they're in the wrong place."

"And where do you tell them is the right place for them?" I asked.

"Oh, they'll get a strong sense of that on their own, once they get that it's time to move on," Helen replied. "That's why you often find them all bundled up with their hat and coat on and maybe holding a bag. They know on some level that they should embark on a journey. They'll find the way on their own normally, once they're fully conscious of their real condition. It must feel awkward and uncomfortable for them to be as stuck as they are. When they're ready, they'll be happy to leave on their own, and it'll be easy for them."

"So they're confused a lot of the time?" I asked.

"Yes," Helen answered.

"Then what if they refuse to leave and refuse to communicate with you?" I asked. "What if they become hostile and belligerent?"

"Okay, then it gets more challenging," Helen admitted. "But there are little tricks you can do. There are tools, so to speak."

"Such as. . . ?" I prodded.

"Such as stakes, holy water, salt, and mirrors," Helen said. "These are common and seem to work for a lot of people."

"Like a stake through the heart?" I asked, thinking of vampire movies.

She laughed. "People sometimes drive big stakes into the corners of a property that's haunted," she explained.

I asked whether *she* had ever found it necessary to stake the grounds of a haunted building.

She shook her head. "Mostly, these are deceased people who want to move on, but for some reason—known only to themselves perhaps—they can't do so or they're too scared to do it. They're just unsettled."

When I quizzed her a bit more about staking out haunted grounds, she said that the stakes should be driven into the four corners of the property, deep into the ground. As one did this, one should call upon the four cardinal directions, acknowledging them as powers or watchtowers. Then, apparently, the spirits should be ordered to leave.

"Don't some people refer to the four cardinal points or watchtowers as the four archangels?" I asked.

Helen nodded in the affirmative.

I commented that, in the past, I had simply ordered spirits to leave my presence, and they had vanished without the need of any tricks.

"For good?" she asked.

"I believe so," I replied. "I never saw them again."

She said that salting haunted grounds was similar to staking grounds. In this case, salt is poured all around the property in one continuous line, which spirits can't cross. "You salt the ground and then order them to leave," she said. "You say that out loud."

"Any particular type of salt?" I asked.

"Don't know that it would matter," she said. "I would use a kosher salt or even a good-quality sea salt."

Her description of the holy water employed was somewhat similar, although the water was to be tossed in the direction that the spirit seemed to be lurking or where its presence was sensed the strongest.

I asked Helen where I might find holy water, and she asked me whether I was Catholic. When I indicated that I wasn't, that abruptly ended the discussion on holy water.

"So what if *none* of that works?" I asked. "And the spirit continues haunting and refusing to comply?"

Helen insisted that was pretty unlikely.

"You also mentioned the use of mirrors," I reminded her. "How do they work?"

"Mirror magick," she mused. "Not for beginners."

I asked what she meant by that.

"I just mean that mirrors are not as simple as they seem. There's a certain mystery to them. You can get lost in a mirror. Do you know anything about mirror magick?" she asked me.

I said I did not.

"Well, a mirror could be used as a last resort for a spirit unwilling to leave, I suppose. I've never had to use one, though. And I doubt that you would either."

We spoke for a while about mirrors, but my lack of knowledge about mirror magick sort of got in the way, and Helen dropped the subject.

I smiled a thank-you to her, then glanced at my written questions, fearing for a moment that I might have forgotten an important question and would never see Helen again.

"Those are not the important questions," she told me point-blank, covering my paper with one hand. "If you want to try de-ghosting a few houses, you'll do fine. Do you have any places in mind?"

I answered in the negative but added that ghosts seemed to find me wherever I went. But now, thanks to Helen, I would be able to deal with them in a more constructive way.

Then something else occurred to me—something darker.

"Wait, I do have a question," I told her. "What about spirits that turn out not to be ghosts at all? What if I were to come across something that's not a deceased person? What if it turns out to be something else entirely?"

Without changing her expression, Helen waved her hand, as though the concern was small and insignificant to her.

"As I said earlier," she said, "you might occasionally stumble on something that's not an actual ghost. That type of energy is formed by the negative emotions of the people who live in the house. It wouldn't be your personal responsibility to get rid of that. It's up to the people who created the thoughtform to dissolve it."

That was a relief to me, and before we left the breakfast table I mentioned to Helen what Louis had told me the night before about finding the right spirits and avoiding the confusion of dark spirits that might try to enter our world. I could see, of course, that Helen's work with ghosts was somewhat simplified compared to the work of Louis, a trance medium who traveled to busy psychic crossroads where a wide array of characters was waiting to interact with him. Helen, on the other hand, worked on the Earth plane, walking into actual houses and dealing exclusively with ghosts who were stuck in the physical world.

On the way out of the inn that morning, I stopped by the front desk to buy Louis's latest book. I then left it with the desk clerk, asking him to ask Louis to autograph it for me, given that I might not see Louis again before our departure for the mainland.

My two companions and I took a final walk up the beach and then through the island bookstore up the road before checking out of the inn. In the harbor we sat on a wooden bench, waiting for the island shuttle to take us to the ferry dock some eight miles away. There wasn't much to say. My friends were probably bored and tired and ready to leave. I, on the other hand, was excited by all that I'd heard and learned from both Helen and Louis. On a productive visit to the island, I might be able to meet with Louis for a few brief moments. This time I had been able to sit down and speak with him at length. Moreover, I had also met his fascinating secretary, Helen.

What a weekend it had been!

The Washington state ferry pulled out from the dock at 2:20 p.m., leaving ducks and seagulls in its wake. As it churned up the straits back to Anacortes and the mainland, I felt something leaving me. It was a little bit of island magic slipping away. I had felt so warmly protected and confident in the presence of my mentors on the island. Now that I had left them both in the wake of the boat, I was beginning to feel empty and alone.

4
Ghost Hunting
at an
Old Portland Church

Subsequent to that trip to Orcas Island, I had no further opportunity to speak with Helen and learn from her. After my early years working for the newspaper in Anacortes, where we'd started the *San Juanderer* summer magazine, I left the area to bounce around the country working for various news outlets. Any further visits to Orcas Island would be sporadic and rare. On the odd occasion when I did manage a visit, I would be lucky to find Louis in residence, but more often than not he was away. Helen was never there when I returned.

I didn't encounter any ghosts or ghostly spirits for some time after my training with Helen. I had mixed feelings about this, although I did feel confident, based on her advice, that I would be able to handle a haunting should one happen to come my way. Then I found myself back in Oregon working for another newspaper. There was definitely something about the Mount Hood area that held my interest. One day I heard about an odd haunting that I thought I should investigate. My friends also agreed that I should check it out. It sounded a bit anomalous, because it didn't involve a haunted house but rather a haunted church.

Made of ancient red bricks, it was one of the oldest churches in the Portland area. As far as I could tell, the property on which it stood stretched from city sidewalk to city sidewalk, with no room for church grounds as the church itself occupied the entire block. The building felt like hallowed ground when one approached it.

I personally knew people from the congregation who were very worried that the church might be haunted, which seemed unthinkable and almost an abomination. The idea that little old ladies and children might be afraid to walk down hallways and go into empty rooms alone in their sacred space was repugnant to these folks.

So I offered to help, in a very unofficial capacity. I didn't approach the church elders, board, clergy, or administrative staff. I went to the church with a work colleague of mine—who was also a member of the church—on a Saturday, a day when very few people were apt to be there. I prepared a bag full of the tools of the trade, so to speak, to take with me.

How long had this old building been haunted? How many people had been deterred by the haunting? I could scarcely wait to get inside to make contact with and remove the ghost.

My friend drove us to the church in a big Buick owned by our newspaper group. We parked across the street from the building, in a parking lot that had been fenced off with "No Trespassing" signs. I didn't think that would prove to be a problem, however, because it was a quiet Saturday and the lot was directly across from the church.

I handed my gym bag full of secret tools to my companion to imply that he should come with me. I wanted some company when I entered the daunting old building. I figured I'd be alone soon enough but didn't want to walk into the strange building all by myself.

Then it hit me that I wouldn't be completely alone as I searched for the ghost. It would be there too; I could be certain about that.

A few minutes after we'd entered the church my companion thrust the gym bag quickly at me and then ran back to the Buick. Perhaps he didn't want to stay to see the ghost . . . I don't know. So as not to frighten anyone that may have been in the church, I sneaked my way around its hallways and then from room to room. But I saw no one. Lights were on here and there, but that was it.

The place was deathly quiet.

I clutched my bag of tricks in one hand and hoped that I wouldn't need them. Ideally, I'd contact the ghost, communicate with it, and convince it to leave. But, again, I didn't sense a thing. I didn't feel a cold or tingling sensation, nor did I hear anything strange. *Nothing* caught my attention. So I continued walking through the large building. I figured that there had to be other people in it given that it was unlocked and, as mentioned, a few lights were on. Maybe I just kept missing whoever was in there. In any event, I felt as though I had entered a maze.

Finally, in the basement, I walked into a room in a far corner of the building. Its door was slightly ajar and I pushed it open and, entering, walked over to the room's sole chair and slowly sat down in it. The door was still cracked halfway open; the hallway providing the only light in the dim room. I sat there, trying to get very still inside of myself. Here was a likely place for me to get in touch with my mystery ghost. Everything was very dark. I was slowly tuning out distractions and inner thoughts and trying to tune in to whatever spirit might be present, just below the surface of my awareness.

I was going deeper and deeper inside myself, stifling normal thoughts and muting sensory impressions from the area around me. I was getting to my deepest level of awareness and was beginning to feel an inner peace and stillness. Fleeting images in my imagination were dissolving, and I began to see a blank screen inside my mind's eye and I stared at it . . . waiting . . . waiting . . . waiting . . .

Suddenly something jarred me. My body twitched, and I opened my eyes, bolting upright in one quick motion. What? Where? My head swiveled around, all five senses instantly alert and wary of what might be out there.

I saw nothing. I was still alone in the dark basement room. Then I heard a clicking sound. It was faint, then grew louder. Something was approaching. It might be footsteps. I slowly arose from the chair and turned toward the half-open doorway. The sound was coming from down the hall.

It occurred to me then and there that I might not really be up for de-ghosting buildings. I put one foot forward and then another, walking slowly toward the door that stood slightly ajar. Then I stood on my side of the door, with one hand on it, almost afraid to look into the hallway. I waited, hoping my next move would be determined for me so that I wouldn't have to commit to any ill-advised course of action.

The clicking sound drew closer and closer, but I couldn't bring myself to look down the hallway just yet. When the sound appeared to be almost upon me, I looked out the door, bracing myself for whatever might come.

It was a man. A building custodian, I determined. He wore dirty work clothes and carried a push broom with him. He was merely a man with a broom—nothing too threatening. I could certainly handle him.

Not expecting me to be there, he walked right past the door and continued on down the hall. Everything was quiet except for the clicking of his heels. He clearly hadn't noticed my presence, and although I wasn't trying to hide from him, I saw no reason to confront him, either. After all, nobody expected me to be down there. So staying in the dark was probably best all around. The janitor might not even know the church was haunted; maybe he was somewhat insensitive to things going on around him.

Once he had cleared the hallway and disappeared into the recesses of the basement, I decided to explore upstairs some more, for I had sensed nothing paranormal downstairs. I tiptoed up the stairway, going all the way to the top of the large building. I reached a sort of loft or balcony from which I could look down into the main sanctuary. Like much of the church that I'd explored earlier, it was unlit and silent.

I sat in a balcony chair and looked down at the altar. There were lights on at the front of the worship area, and I could see a chart with numbers on it. The numbers no doubt were a tally of attendees at the previous Sunday's service. On the other side of the altar was a similar chart that appeared to have dates on it. I was unable to make out much more.

Then it dawned on me that I was focusing on the sanctuary below but paying no attention to the area where I was seated. I looked around slowly, turning my head only slightly. It was a large seating area that could accommodate more than a hundred people. There were rows and rows of chairs—I couldn't see much more than that. The lighting was so dim that someone could be seated at the end of the balcony and I probably wouldn't be able to see him or her.

I closed my eyes and settled in my chair to try to tune in to any other presence that might be there in the darkness. I grounded myself by placing both feet flat and snug on the floor. I improved my posture so that my spine was straight. I put my hands to my sides so that they weren't restrained. I worked to clear my head and to reach a quiet, still point deep within.

A blank screen began to form in my mind's eye. I focused on this blank screen, trying to sense things on a different level. I waited to pick up a sound or a signal or an image that might come to me, but after a few minutes of this, I wondered how long I should wait, for I saw and heard nothing. I was not tuning in to anything, and I began to grow impatient.

I opened my eyes and looked around again, afraid that in so doing I would be letting my guard down, thereby inviting trouble. And yet, still there was nothing.

Perhaps I simply wasn't very good at making contact, or maybe my ghost didn't want to make itself known and was therefore avoiding me.

I opened my gym bag, which contained the tools I'd brought

with me to deal with difficult ghosts. Inside were four large stakes (seven-inch penny spikes that were actually big enough to nail railroad ties together), a box of unopened kosher salt, and a little glass bottle that I thought would suffice for holding holy water. I had no holy water at home, and figured I might find some at the church as the occasion demanded.

Just then I heard something at the end of the balcony near the stairway. I zipped the bag closed and rose slowly from my chair. I walked quietly to the end of the balcony and leaned to look down the stairs. I saw a light at the bottom of the stairway. It raced across the hallway that opened onto the staircase, then stopped. I froze, not knowing what to do or expect. Then the light flashed across the opening to the stairway again.

I inched downstairs. During my descent, the area was dark. When I reached the bottom, the light returned.

I twisted my head to look around the staircase wall and down the hallway. Nothing. I looked in the other direction and saw a man with a flashlight. It was the custodian again. I remained where I was until he left. When I heard a heavy door close, I figured our custodian was done for the day.

I entered the hallway and retraced my steps to the front entry doors. I didn't see or hear anyone along the way. I paused before the doors to the immense church. Had I managed to get myself locked inside the church? I wondered with dismay.

Pulling on the doors confirmed my worst fears. I was indeed locked inside the church. I thought about my friend in the Buick as someone who could help me. But I had no way of contacting him, and he didn't have keys to the church. How long would I be in here? I wondered. Well, there would be services on Sunday morning, but that meant I would have to spend the night alone in the church.

I started wandering through the building again, assuming that I wouldn't encounter any other people now that it was locked. At least there would be no need to dodge anyone or hide from the custodian in order not to have to explain my presence here, I reasoned.

I was kicking myself for being in this predicament. In hindsight I decided that perhaps I should have been more upfront about my intentions from the get-go. I should have gone to the church office and told the staff what I wanted to do, so that they could have given me clearance and set up a time for me to conduct my inquiry. At least then I wouldn't be locked up in a haunted church at the end of the day.

I found the cafeteria and the kitchen, which had huge ovens and huge sinks and counter space. I opened one of the large double-door refrigerators to find something cool to drink. I found nothing.

Rummaging through a nearby cupboard, I found a packet of cherry drink mix and dumped it into a pitcher, and then added water and ice cubes to make myself a cold drink. As I was bending over to retrieve a cube of ice I'd dropped on the floor, a strange sound broke my concentration, and I dropped the whole ice tray. The ice cubes cracked like glass on the floor, scattering ice chips in every direction.

I moved out into the cafeteria, looking for the source of the sound. Was this my ghost?

My search took me to the basement where a window opening to the back lot was banging back and forth in the wind. I examined the window, and although it was small (and built before current building codes required egress accommodations) I figured that I might be able to squeeze out through its opening.

Like everything else in the old church, though, the window was rusty and hard to open all the way. It was one of those old-style lead and frosted glass windows from the past century, and I wanted to avoid breaking it. Because it was about four or five feet off the ground, I'd need a chair or something else to stand on in order to get through it. Once I had the window wide open and the chair firmly in place, I stuffed my body through its tiny opening.

I then fell like a stone. The hard asphalt of the back parking lot met my descent four or five feet below. There were no cars in the lot. Neither had anyone seen my great escape, and for that I was grateful. I was there to de-ghost the glorious old church, not to break and enter it, which is no doubt how things might look to anyone happening by.

I walked across the street to my friend in the Buick, and, as I approached the car, he rolled down his window.

"So where's the gym bag?" he asked me.

I had totally forgotten about the gym bag, and then remembered that I'd also left the cherry drink mess in the kitchen. Yes, I had to return, if only to clean up my mess and retrieve the bag. So I left my friend in the Buick and returned to the church.

Getting back through the window was harder from the outside, because the opening was off the ground and I had no chair to boost me up to the proper height. So I rummaged around and found a large rock to stand on. I was careful not to break the window and ended up doing a sort of a somersault onto the basement floor of the church on re-entry.

I found my gym bag and then rushed back to clean up the kitchen.

This was getting quite silly. Was there really a ghost? Maybe the old building just creaked and felt cold to people from time to time, and they thought it was spooky when wandering through it alone. We can frighten ourselves if we let our imaginations run wild, I thought. After all, I had been frightened by the footsteps of a mere custodian walking down the hall.

Maybe I was just trying to talk myself out of approaching the ghost by rationalizing that it didn't exist. Was my reluctance simply attributable to the fact that I wanted to avoid a scary confrontation in the old building? With this thought I resolved to move forward and to check out every room and corner of the building.

To that end I opened door after door in that old church. I looked behind the sanctuary, in the area near the sanctuary where the choir and speakers gather, and in the library. I even looked in the nursery and then walked through many rooms that looked to be classrooms. Then there were dusty broom closets and storage areas to explore. I just kept walking through the cavernous building, trying very hard to clear my head and tune in to any sensations or a presence that might be there.

Thus far, however, I wandered alone, and was left to my own inner thoughts.

Not a thing came to me, even though I tried sitting very quietly in some of the rooms, listening for something—anything!

Was the ghost hiding, perhaps?

I opened the gym bag on the floor by my feet. What tools could I use here? What tricks would trip up my sly ghost who now appeared to be concealing itself, unwilling to be seen or confronted?

Looking through the bag, I had to admit that perhaps the problem was me. Maybe I lacked the proper sensitivity to make contact with a ghost. Maybe this ghost had actually walked with me every step of the way, but I just couldn't sense it! Stakes, salt, a mirror, and an empty bottle for holy water were in my bag. I could look in the church for the holy water I lacked, but I wasn't in a Catholic church and I wondered how I might find water that had been sanctified or blessed in a way that might make a difference.

I hadn't been trained in the use of a mirror.

That left only the stakes and the salt.

The salt, I knew, should be applied to the grounds around the building. The same went for the stakes. So I zipped the gym bag shut and returned to the basement window.

I propped the chair back under the open window again, and again I fell onto the parking lot's hard pavement. Although it was becoming dark, it wasn't yet dark enough for any streetlights or security lights to have been triggered near the church. However, it was dark enough that I had a bit of cover in which to move without being detected. I walked around the building, which took quite awhile given its immense size.

When I'd finished, I found myself across the street from the Buick. Walking over to my friend, I tapped on his window to get him to roll down the glass. Either he had dozed off or was absorbed in the radio. I couldn't tell which, but I startled him.

"Couldn't find your ghost on the inside anywhere!" I told him. "I'm going to work outside now."

"Doing what?" he asked.

"Well, I can salt and stake the grounds," I told him. "I have both."

"Will that do it, then?" he asked. He had never met Helen, so he was unfamiliar with the drill. But then maybe I hadn't fully grasped it, either. I had never really communicated with a ghost or de-ghosted a building before. I was just copying the routine of a woman I'd met briefly, following her instructions as best I could recall them.

"Stay here," I told my friend. "I don't need your help."

"What a relief!" he replied, rolling up the car window.

I walked slowly around the building one more time, looking for a place where I should start. It all felt about the same. I felt nothing, except very empty and alone.

Finally, I came to the northwest corner of the church. Nobody was around, making it a good place to start. Yes, I *was* somewhat self-conscious and thought myself a little bit silly. What the heck was I doing here when there was no ghost to be found? Why was I going to all this trouble?

I knelt on one knee and zipped open the bag. A large stake lay on top, and I lifted it out. Because the walk was made of concrete, I dithered about where to sink it into the ground; there was no soft dirt. Finally, I decided to slip the stake into the edge of the sidewalk on the side of the building where a gap left just enough space for the girth of the spike.

I pushed the spike into the ground, but it wouldn't penetrate the surface because the soil was too hard. I gave it another push, but no luck. I looked in the gym bag in search of something I might use as a protective cover over the spike so that I could pound the spike with an open palm. Nothing appropriate was inside the bag.

Looking around, I found a rock. It could have been larger, but it would work. I used this primitive tool to pound the spike into the ground. At last, the spike was down almost flush with the pavement. It wouldn't stick out and become uprooted by anyone anytime soon. I tossed the rock into the gym bag and walked around the building to the next corner. I knelt and sank a spike into that corner, using the rock again. I rounded the building to the third corner, where I repeated the procedure, and then did the same with the fourth and final corner.

As I sank the final spike into the fourth cardinal point, I paused as though expecting to hear or experience something. Maybe ghosts become upset and defiant when their habitats are spiked, I reasoned. I zipped the bag shut and rose to my feet, the bag firmly in hand. In the other hand I held the rock, which I then tossed toward the building. It sparked as it skidded across the sidewalk.

All of a sudden a loud popping sound greeted my ears. It sounded like a gunshot! Then I saw an old wreck of a car driving in my direction on the street adjacent to the old church. I sighed with relief. A car had backfired, nothing more, I reasoned with myself. I smiled and patted the bag with a sense of slight satisfaction.

Back at the Buick, my friend wasn't so satisfied.

"Well, how can you be sure that you got him?" he challenged me. "You didn't see anything at all?"

"No," I replied.

"Then you never found the ghost, never confronted him, and never banished him," he told me.

Suddenly *he* was the expert! Suddenly, *he* knew all about ghosts! I gave him a dirty look, for I'd done everything I could.

"Are you sure you did everything you could?" he asked, as though reading my mind. "Did you use every tool in your bag?"

I took inventory in my head. I hadn't used the mirror and I didn't have any holy water. I could have used the salt, but I hadn't.

"Well, I could salt the grounds before we leave, just to be certain," I said. "But honestly, I didn't pick up on anything at all anywhere in the building or outside. I don't think the building's haunted."

"It is," he insisted. "It's been haunted forever. Lots of people have seen its ghost."

"Have *you*?" I asked him.

"Not exactly," he said, "but I've met plenty of people who've had some bad experiences that they really don't want to talk about."

"Okay, okay," I said. "Just to be safe, I'll salt the building. I'll place kosher salt all around it and at its four corners. Feel better now?"

He smiled and rolled the window back up.

Some help he is, I fumed.

I returned to where I had placed the first spike and bent over again to unzip the bag.

My box of kosher salt was unopened, so I punched in the pour spout. I stood up and started spreading a steady stream of salt from the corner down along the sidewalk. Walking around the building, I visited its other three cardinal points and sprinkled all of my salt out onto the ground in one narrow stream. I then stood back to admire my handiwork.

There. The building had been salted. According to Helen, that should repel the ghost.

As I placed the empty salt box into the gym bag, something caught my attention out of the corner of my eye. For an instant, it almost looked like a light had flickered on in one of the upper rooms of the church. But looking across at the gigantic building now, the entire church looked dark and deserted.

Perhaps it had just been my imagination. On the other hand, I really didn't want to hang around any longer to find out.

I don't know to this day, really, who or what haunted the church or whether the reports by some church members and visitors were actual sightings or simply fabrications of their imaginations. Maybe there was a deceased custodian who haunted the building at certain times. I never heard again from the friend who had accompanied me to the church, so maybe he decided that there was no real spook in the building after all. I am not so sure, because I did detect flickering lights that could not be explained. And being in that building did give me a creepy feeling during my inspection. Some ghosts, it must be said, are pretty good at hiding and avoiding people. Perhaps this church had a reclusive ghost of little harm to anyone.

5
Mutilations, Floating Heads, and a Talking Dead Girl

After my visit to the old Portland church I thought nothing more about ghosts for some time. Certainly, my one big day as a ghost hunter had produced nothing to get very excited about. Maybe I just didn't have it in me to de-ghost buildings. Maybe there weren't that many ghosts haunting us, but rather unsubstantiated *rumors* of ghosts.

My work in Oregon at the newspaper kept me busy enough, for we had lots of real things to worry about. Sure, it was a sleepy little mountain community on Mount Hood, but there was no shortage of drama and disaster of the everyday sort. We had horrible traffic accidents on the mountain pass, fires, lost hikers, and political infighting. Or maybe I just experienced it all more personally because I covered the news for the local rag.

One strange story that mesmerized us that summer involved a small group of ladies who reportedly performed healings in a chapel in the woods near a place called Sleepy Hollow. Although it was close to my home, I had never visited it. Many of the small religious communities on the mountain met in houses or cabins. At one such church service

I attended I sat in a laundry room next to the clothes dryer. The people of this rural community were mountain folks, the descendants of Oregon pioneers, and many of them were colorful individuals indeed.

We started hearing funny stories about the chapel in the woods, but no one at the paper had ever met anyone associated with it. The chapel appeared to be private; its organizers never listed their services in our directory of church activities or provided any kind of news about their upcoming meetings. Most places liked free publicity and wanted to attract visitors. Not the chapel in the woods.

You would hear people speculating about what might be taking place there, but not even the local gossips seemed to have any solid slant on it. I would hear about the chapel's leaders coming into town from time to time, which made me think that perhaps they weren't all that secretive after all.

One day a lady from the chapel came into our newspaper office and asked how to donate to a local charity she'd heard about. Her group wanted to support a burn victim who'd gotten much too close to his backyard propane grill with a leaky gas line. I gave her the contact information she requested, and she left without really introducing herself or saying anything about her group.

Nice lady, I thought to myself, although she's very secretive even in her public display of support.

One person in our town who claimed to be psychic said the woman from the chapel appeared to be surrounded by a huge energy bubble of purple light as she walked down the street. Personally, I failed to see anything like that when she dropped by our office and concluded that although I hadn't seen her walking through town, psychics are apt to make all sorts of outlandish claims.

We had a mountain correspondent who wanted to check out the chapel in the woods. Marshall was an enterprising young man who worked for us part-time and was paid by the amount of space he could fill in our paper with mountain news from far up the hill, way out of town. He covered hidden places like Sleepy Hollow. He was always looking for a new controversy in some remote place where nobody might think to look.

When Marshall told me that he wanted to check out the chapel in the woods and maybe even write an article about it, I gave him approval to do so. I also realized that his excursion might not amount to anything, given that it might be the case that the chapel's members would refuse to open up about themselves. It was my opinion that the ladies in the woods probably didn't want a newspaper article written about their little group, given their lack of interest in publicizing when their services were held.

It took Marshall quite awhile to determine when the ladies would be in attendance. I believe he knocked on a few doors in Sleepy Hollow to try to find this out. Turns out nobody knew much more than he did, but finally some neighbor figured out when the chapel was in use, just by being nosy and keeping one eye open.

Chatting with Marshall before his adventure in the woods, I really didn't expect him to take notes on his little expedition. He was known to shun details like that when he went undercover. Marshall's approach in this case was to visit the chapel and pretend he was sick with a disease that the doctors couldn't quite diagnose. He would then ask the ladies to heal him. I really didn't believe we would get anything from this whole thing except for Marshall's impressions. And I figured that wouldn't fit into anything like a genuine news article, even as a colorful feature. But it would be interesting, at least, to hear what story he might bring back to us.

We were therefore a bit surprised when Marshall returned the next morning with his frightening tale about what the ladies in the chapel in the woods had done to him. Apparently they had welcomed him into the wooden chapel and told him that they used light to heal people. Marshall was waiting for this healing light to strike him and cover him with radiance and warmth.

What actually took place, however, had been much more physical and emotionally jarring. He said that the women started to sing and chant and took turns sitting on him. Mostly, they sat on his hands, but at times several of the women piled atop him and covered his arms and legs. He said that they rolled around on him and bruised him. Allegedly all of this was pretty painful, even for a rugged mountain man like Marshall who said he had no interest in interviewing these women, writing about their chapel in the woods, or ever visiting them again. After his personal ordeal, Marshall said he could hardly wait to get out of there.

I quizzed him a little but didn't get much more out of him than that. He offered no names or details about how the chapel operated. It was just a rustic chapel in the middle of the woods with dim lighting and a bunch of eccentric old ladies. At least, that was the abbreviated story Marshall told me, and it was clear from his attitude that he didn't want to talk about it any longer. I think he just wanted to forget the whole thing.

I too might have forgotten all about the spiritual ladies in the woods if it hadn't been for the fact that one weekend soon thereafter a young lady knocked on the door of my Brightwood home. Frankly, I had no idea who she was. There were only about a dozen of us living in the neighborhood, which was a relatively new development carved out of an old-growth forest near the Salmon River. I pretty much knew my neighbors. She was not one of us.

She was frantic when she pounded on my door, bypassing the doorbell entirely. When I opened the door, she fell into the living room and immediately started talking nonstop. I tried calming her down and learned that her name was Laura. She had been staying with her boyfriend at one of the new houses around the corner. She wanted to move out right away and get back to Portland. And she wanted to use my phone.

I ushered her into the kitchen where my phone was on the wall, and she picked up its receiver and dialed a number. I couldn't hear her conversation, given that she spoke in halting, hushed tones. When she was finished, I invited her to sit on the sofa and collect herself.

Laura had lived in Brightwood for just a few months, she told me. She had moved up originally to look for her sister, who had been missing since early spring. Her sister was named Diane, and apparently they were close in age. I guessed that to be mid-twenties. She told me that her sister had spent some time on the mountain, picking mushrooms and hiking, and had met a few people this way. For the most part, Laura had no idea who these people were, with the exception of some folks that Diane had told Laura about: a mysterious group of women in the woods who had a little chapel and performed healings—light healings, she called them.

Now this sounded familiar to me as I flashed back to Marshall's adventure, so I asked Laura if they met in a sort of rustic chapel in the woods. Her eyes were wild and she nodded excitedly, apparently glad to talk to somebody who had some idea what she was talking about.

She said these people in the woodsy chapel seemed to keep to themselves but had taken Diane into their midst. Apparently, Diane had found the prospect of healing with light promising. Laura explained that her sister was a bit troubled but was really just searching for some sort of anchor in her life. From Marshall's description of the chapel in the woods, I didn't think Diane would find much stability there.

Laura closed her eyes, as though to gather herself a bit.

"The thing is," she said, "I got a call from Diane not long ago. I don't know how she knew the number at the house here, but that's where I got the call. It was the strangest call I've ever received. She sounded so scared, almost incoherent. I had trouble understanding her at first. Then I realized that it was Diane. She said, 'Laurie, it's me! It's me! You've got to help me, Laurie! They won't let me go! I'm scared for my life. Really. You've got to believe me!'"

Laura said that the line went dead before she could learn any more so she couldn't ascertain where her sister was or what trouble she might be in. This information was making Laura crazy, but, try as she might, she couldn't get her boyfriend or any of their friends to share her concerns. It seems that they didn't take the call seriously, implying that perhaps Laura had fabricated it or imagined it somehow, or that maybe it was some sort of a prank call.

Suddenly Laura arose and said she had to go. I thought she was about to ask me to help her find her sister. Instead, she urged me to take some furniture off her hands. Apparently, she'd designed and crafted all of her own furniture. Given that she was leaving the area, she wanted to dispose of it before she left, and, to that end, she'd brought a custom-made secretarial desk to my house. It was sitting outside my door as I checked it out. It was a nice piece, and I decided to keep it. After thanking Laura and encouraging her to stay in touch, I gave her my name and phone number. And with that, she left.

Really, I had no idea why she'd knocked on my door, because she hadn't connected me with the newspaper and didn't know me from Adam. It was probably that my house was the only nearby house with a light shining in the window.

I hauled her flip-top secretarial desk upstairs to my bedroom, and, after I put it into a vacant corner, I gave little thought to Laura's story. Young people like her sister drifted through our mountain community all the time, escaping the hubbub of the city and looking to find themselves somewhere in the pristine darkness of the national forest. I assumed that Diane would turn up somewhere when her sister least expected it. Young people without an anchor are like that, I told myself.

It was strange about her sister's involvement with the chapel in the woods, however. I wondered whether it was the same one that Marshall had visited, although that would be quite a coincidence. But maybe she had met the same ladies in the woods, and they had tried their healing magic on her. Because there were no reports of missing people in our area, though, I didn't worry too much about Laura's wayward sister. Any reports of missing people, foul play, or accidents on the mountain would have been relayed by our local authorities to the newspaper and would have crossed my desk. That was not the case here.

A few days later Laura was loading some personal items onto the bed of a truck at her boyfriend's house. I watched them from my front window. She was moving mostly clothes and some furniture from what I could see, and she appeared to be arguing with her boyfriend through the whole procedure, with him shouting back at her. Clearly this was not a friendly parting. It occurred to me that Laura was perhaps a little unstable like her sister. On the other hand, this was none of my business, and I intended to keep it that way.

My newspaper job at the bottom of the mountain kept me busy enough for the next day or two. That summer seemed to have its share of strange events and mishaps. We had a tractor trailer overturn on Highway 26, apparently after skidding on wet leaves. (Long-haul truckers on the mountain pass were known to pass through our part of the world in a somewhat sleep-deprived condition.) We also had the typical barn fire and lost-hiker stories to cover on Mount Hood. In the winter the mountain took its toll on skiers. In the summer it also took its toll on climbers and foolhardy hikers who overlooked the fact that the mountain sported a permanent ice-capped glacier. There was a good reason why the U.S. and Canadian Olympic ski teams trained on it off-season.

Then an odd piece of mystery crossed the news desk. There were reports that near Hoodland, which was a community a bit higher up the mountain, birds were being slaughtered and dumped in public places. One of the reports came from the Hoodland Volunteer Fire Department and another from the Welches school district.

The fire department was dispatched on a rather unusual 911 call that reported decapitated birds floating in a lake in their jurisdiction. This was a park at the extreme end of the county—a county that had no police department. Although they were hardly police investigators, the firefighters had been dispatched to check out the report. Indeed, they found dead birds that, in addition to having been slaughtered, had also been mutilated. All were large birds; they included an eagle. The firemen were the most concerned about the eagle, because it's a protected species and a revered sight to behold in flight in the pristine wilds of our mountain. It was unclear from the report just what the other birds might be. I was thinking crows, but our area was also home to wild grouse and quail, which were frequently seen along the glacier-fed river that ran down the mountain.

The fire department was also concerned about the wanton destruction of wildlife and desecration at a local public park. In the weeks ahead they would work with the national foresters of the ranger station at the Mount Hood National Forest to design and distribute fliers to alert people to what had transpired and request information from anyone who might know something more about these incidents.

The similar matter at the Welches Elementary School really had the local school board and administration concerned. Once again, birds had been mutilated. This time, however, they had been run up the flagpole. The sight of savagely slaughtered birds flapping at the top of the flagpole had not reached many young eyes, fortunately, because school was out for the summer. A custodian of the grounds had noticed blood dripping from the pole when he was cutting the grass nearby. The huge U.S. flag had been removed, too, which had school officials pretty upset.

The scene at the school was still pretty gruesome when a couple of us from the newspaper raced up there to take a few photos and look around. Nothing had been cleaned up or even touched but instead had been left intact—as though it was a crime scene. Well, I suppose it *was* a crime scene, but because the birds had no personal rights, it was more a case of public destruction. Being nature lovers, most mountain folks—including our staff—saw it as murder.

Outside of the school by the flagpole we encountered the superintendent of the tiny one-school district. He was a middle-aged man who wore a gray-checkered sports jacket and black tie even in summer. We called him Cactus Jack, but never to his face. His whole life was that grade school, and he took no vacations from it.

"Just horrible!" Jack hissed without really looking our way. His eyes were glued to the top of the flagpole.

"Is anyone going to lower the birds to the ground?" I asked the superintendent.

He just continued to stare at the dead birds up the pole without responding. Then he abruptly walked away, as though he was thoroughly disgusted by the whole situation. He began pacing in circles around the parking lot, which was normally filled with a lot of teachers' cars but was pretty empty on this sad day.

It was plain to everybody that the superintendent was absorbed in thoughts of a dark nature and didn't care to field any questions just then.

The officers on the scene directed the custodian to work the flagpole chain and lower the birds to the ground. Once on the cement, they looked even more gruesome than they had at a slight distance. You could see slash marks on them, and their heads had been cut off, as well as their talons.

"Who would do something like this?" I asked one of the two officers. "Any ideas? Anybody see or report anything?"

He just shook his head. He and his partner were Clackamas County sheriff's deputies who were assigned to cover our remote corner of the county, and this sort of thing was outside their typical range of experience.

After they had bagged the remains of the birds and cleaned up the parking lot (blood still stained the cement), they quietly put everything in the trunk of their patrol car and then sat in the front seat, writing up a report. They wrote slowly, as though the right words weren't coming easily to them.

I'd been at the scene of a double decapitation on Highway 26 one dark, wet spring afternoon a few months earlier when these same two deputies had bagged the remains of a couple of young men. The victims had been drinking before they ran over a metal barrier that marked a corner in the road, which they had failed to negotiate successfully. As grisly as that scene had been, with steam rising from the severed bodies, on that occasion these two deputies seemed less affected and more talkative than they appeared at the school grounds.

There was something especially upsetting about people who would intentionally and cruelly dismember birds and then put their work on display. It was a crime against nature and in that, it was completely abhorrent.

Back at the newspaper office I turned in my film for processing, not particularly proud of the photos I'd taken. Maybe I should have shown a little restraint by *not* photographing the mutilation of the birds in such graphic close-up. In any event, I wrote captions for my pictures and then coded the photos to run with the story. Only I didn't have much of a story at this point. My plan was to check with the sheriff's office to read what the deputies had filed by way of a report. Maybe they'd investigate and have more information the next morning.

When I called for an official county update the following day, however, I was surprised to learn that there was quite a bit more to the story than I'd originally thought. While investigating other bird mutilations up at the lake a few miles from the school, the Clackamas County deputies had received more grisly news. Someone had reported the body of a dead person floating in another corner of the lake. Because the body appeared mutilated, the deputies were speculating that the two incidents were possibly related and probably had been done by the same person.

The sheriff's department was withholding most of their information about this discovery until they could identify the body and notify next of kin. No prodding from me could get any more information from them at that point. They did tell me where the body had been found and suggested I contact them again in a day or two when they might be able to tell me more.

I grabbed my camera bag and writing pad and drove up to the lake to see what I could see and maybe talk to some locals. I figured that I could at least get a photo of the spot where the body had reportedly been recovered so that we could run a news shot of it. Maybe that section of the beach had been taped off, which might make for an even better news photo.

I walked around almost the entire lake before I was able to determine that I'd found the right place, given the description of the logs and overhanging limbs that the sheriff's office had provided me with. This was a remote part of the lake, in the weeds, and not accessible by a trail, so I got a little wet and scratched up from wandering around the swampy part of the property. There was no crime-scene tape or other indication that a body had recently been removed from the area.

Nonetheless, I dutifully took a couple of photographs, bracketing up and down with my settings so I'd be certain to have something that was properly exposed and printable.

I wanted to find someone nearby to ask about the incident, hoping that they might have seen the body when it washed ashore or could describe to me how the deputies had recovered it. Maybe I'd even get lucky and find a local who'd witnessed what had happened or had some other clues. Given that I had no real solid information with which to write up a story, I was prepared to print just about any comment that an eyewitness might offer up.

The editor of a community newspaper in a neighboring area on the other side of the mountain was very fond of the quote, "Never let the facts get in the way of a good story." At least that was the colorful statement on a T-shirt he frequently wore. I thought of that quote when I was scrambling to find something to print on this story.

Wandering around the alleged crime scene, I found no houses, cabins, hikers, or swimmers. Then I heard the sound of a small outboard motor from the other end of the lake. As it got closer I waved at the man driving the boat and slowly the craft swerved and started heading my way. When it reached the shore near me, I waded out and grabbed the boat's bow to pull it onto the beach. The old man who was in the boat stood up.

"Thanks," he said to me.

"Say, I'm with the local paper," I replied. "I wonder if you saw the sheriff's deputies pull that body out of the water or know anything about it, anything at all."

He removed his fishing hat and dropped it onto the seat of the boat, collecting his thoughts.

"Yeah," he said. "I was here, fishing. Came over to see what the commotion was all about. Saw the deputies over here. When I came over in the boat, they told me to keep my distance. So I pulled ashore way over there," he said, pointing to a spot up the shoreline. "I watched them for a while. Body looked bad. Decomposed, I guess. And a mess."

"What do you mean?" I asked.

"Well, the body was hacked up or something. Parts missing. Almost didn't look like a person."

"Was it a man, a woman, or a child?" I asked. "Could you tell?"

"Hmm," he hesitated. "A small person, but not a child or small child, I'd say. Slender. Probably a woman."

"Why do you say it was probably a woman?" I prodded.

"Slender build. Not too tall. Very pale and thin."

"Thin build?" I repeated to clarify.

"Yeah, and wasted," he said. "Like she'd lost a lot of blood."

I inquired further, but he couldn't tell me anything more. He'd seen nothing before the officers had arrived, and he'd heard nothing suspicious either.

With his permission, I took his photo, which I would print together with his eyewitness comments; I had little else to build a news article around.

Later in the day, I called the sheriff's department for an update. They couldn't give me any new information but did confirm that the body had bled out. In fact, they said it was as though the body had been drained of *all* its fluids. They thought it was a woman but couldn't know her identity because there were no fingerprints on file that matched. There was also no chance of identification through dental records, because they hadn't recovered the head.

This was another decapitation.

So there was a connection between the body in the lake and the bird mutilations at the lake and the school: decapitation. The crimes appeared to be almost ritualistic, but the sheriff's department spokesman wouldn't comment on that. They did tell me that the body had been in the lake for more than a few days judging by its level of deterioration. When I pressed for a more specific time period, the spokesman would only say that it had been in the lake for several days. Apparently they were awaiting the coroner's final report.

I got to thinking about Laura's sister who had gone missing and wondered whether the dead woman could be her. Finding Laura might prove difficult, I thought to myself, since she'd moved and I didn't have her full name or contact information. The best way to try to contact her would be for me to visit the house of her estranged boyfriend, who probably wouldn't be very helpful, judging by the way they had parted.

When I dropped by his house on my way home that night, he wasn't there. So I left a note with my name and number on it. Later that evening, peering out my window, I saw him return home, but I didn't receive a call from him. So I dropped by his house on my way to work the next morning. He was eating breakfast in the kitchen, but he got up and came to the door. After I told him who I was and that I needed Laura's phone number, he put up one hand as though to minimize our conversation. Then he raised a finger as though to say "wait a minute" and disappeared inside the house. He returned to the door in short order with a slip of paper in his hand on which had been scribbled a phone number. He handed the paper over to me.

"Sorry, I can't help you more," he said. "You can reach her at this number."

Before I could pepper him with questions or even offer thanks, he had closed the door in my face.

I called Laura from my office. She answered on the first ring, as though she'd been sitting right by the phone.

"Laura, it's the guy you gave your secretarial desk to," I said. "I got your phone number from your old boyfriend up here at Brightwood."

"He's not my boyfriend," she replied.

"Yeah, I know," I answered. "Look, I wanted to ask you something about that phone call you got from your sister. Do you remember telling me about it? The strange call?"

"Yes," she said.

"When did you get that call?" I asked her. "Do you remember when she called you?"

"It was just . . . like the day before I saw you," she said. "It was just the other day."

"Not a week ago? More like four or five days ago?"

"Yes. Why?"

"Well, I don't want to alarm you unnecessarily," I said. "And maybe it's not even related. But the sheriff's department has found someone up here."

"Is she okay?" Laura asked excitedly.

"No, no. They found a body. But—look, they haven't even identified the body, so it probably isn't her, you know. I shouldn't have scared you with all of this."

"But you think there might be a connection?" Laura asked.

"Oh, probably not. No, not really. I mean, they don't even know for certain that it's a woman. You can call them yourself if you like—the Clackamas County sheriff's department in Oregon City. Maybe by tomorrow they can straighten out the whole thing. They don't know much at this point. They just found the body."

"And it's a woman?" Laura challenged me.

"Well, no, not for sure," I said. "Maybe not."

"But they just found her in the lake, and my sister called only a few days ago."

"No," I insisted. "This body had been in the lake for some time, so it couldn't be your sister, since she called you about three days ago. This person has been dead longer than that. This person was already dead when you got the call from your sister. See?"

I probably hadn't really comforted Laura after getting her all worked up over the body that had been found in the lake. She was fixated on her missing sister. The woman in the lake had been dead when Diane had called her sister. I told myself that it couldn't be Diane who had been found in the lake.

6
Dealing with the Spirits in My House

It was our mountain correspondent, Marshall, who first suggested a potential link between the mutilations in our community and the chapel in the woods, but of course he was always looking for a way to connect the conspiratorial dots. On occasion, however, he was right. Even so, in this case I cautioned him from making wild accusations about a bunch of old ladies in the woods just because they had upset him and seemed to be a bit eccentric.

The idea of old ladies who ran a chapel and kept to themselves was probably the sort of thing that would stimulate a lot of curiosity, idle chatter, and speculation from some folks. To me, it just seemed irresponsible to start pointing fingers based on what little we knew. These savage killings were surely the work of a madman I told myself—a violent person.

But Laura had said that Diane had visited a chapel in the woods before she'd disappeared. Now I was reasonably certain that Laura's sister was not the person found dead in the lake, given the fact that they had spoken on the phone only recently. And the sheriff's department had told me that the corpse showed signs of decomposition, suggesting that it had been in the lake for some time. Nonetheless, I had to do some poking around on such a big story, because details from the officials were not immediately forthcoming. My readers would want to know anything and everything I could learn before the story became old news.

Toward that end, I decided to visit the chapel in the woods for myself. Marshall was the only person who knew exactly where it was, but sending him up there again was out of the question. He could, however, give me directions to the place and a sense of when might be the best time for a visit.

The map he drew me turned out to be amazingly detailed and accurate, and I was able to find the chapel quite easily, in the middle of a thicket of woods, isolated from any houses or decent roads. I approached what appeared to be a simple cabin slapped together with scrap lumber by semi-skilled hands. Candlelight was flickering in the windows and some frilly colorful images had been painted on the door, making the overall appearance a little less crude. I think they were depictions of wildflowers and mountain herbs. It was just the sort of homey decorations you would expect sweet old ladies nestled in the woods to be crafting in their spare time.

I walked up the four wooden steps to the front door and started to knock. Almost as soon as I had put my fist to the door, however, it sprang open. A squat older woman with silver hair stood in front of me. I recognized her immediately as the woman who had visited the newspaper office to inquire about making a donation to the local charity drive.

"Hello, do you remember me from the newspaper office in town?" I asked her. "We were chatting about making a donation for the burn victim."

She smiled quickly, then her expression reverted to its deadpan look.

Staring right at me, she asked, "Can I help you?"

I was trying to size up whether she was in a cordial mood or not really willing to tolerate strangers on her property. Mountain people could be a bit unsociable at times in their quest for woodsy isolation.

"Ah, yes," I said. "I was looking for a young woman named Diane. Her sister, one of my neighbors, asked whether I'd help locate her. Have you seen a young woman named Diane, probably in her twenties, around here?"

The old woman continued to stare at me blankly.

"There *was* a young woman who came by here the other week. I think her name might have been Diane. She's not here now. She visited the chapel."

"How long did she stay?" I inquired.

The old woman's eyes narrowed slightly and her brow furrowed a bit. "Only briefly," she replied. "Not long. Then she left us. Troubled girl."

"Do you have any more information about her?" I asked. "Her sister is very worried. She hasn't heard from her in some time."

"Not really," she replied.

"Where she might have been going?" I coaxed. "Where she might have been staying up here? Maybe somebody she knew in the area? Anything at all?"

The woman shook her silver hair.

"The sheriff's department has found a body in the lake. They don't know who it is, but it might be that of a young woman," I told her.

"Really!" she said. "And they can't identify the body?"

"Not yet," I said. "Still waiting for the county coroner's complete autopsy."

"Well, I would have no way of knowing anything about any of that," she answered back. "We stay pretty much to ourselves up here."

I tried to peek into the wooden cabin, but she was blocking it for the most part with her middle-aged girth.

"No, she didn't leave anything behind here. Nothing," the woman said.

"Diane?"

"Yes, I believe that was her name. She just dropped by one night but didn't stay very long. Hiking through the area, we thought. Then she left us. Troubled girl."

"Well, you might want to call the sheriff's department in Oregon City and tell them what you can remember about her, such as when she was here and how she looked."

"No phone," she replied.

"Maybe you could use a neighbor's phone," I suggested.

"No neighbors nearby," she said as she extended her heavy arms, which were draped in a purple pullover adorned with glittering silver stars and moons.

"Or I could call *for* you and have a deputy drop by here to take your statement if you like," I said, trying to read her blank expression. She didn't seem very empathetic, but then she *had* said she'd met the girl only briefly.

"I really have nothing to add," she said. She started to close the door at that point.

"But . . ." I blurted out, trying to detain her.

"Thank you for the information," she said to end the conversation. "Good-bye now."

She closed the door on me. Well, I thought to myself, she probably didn't mean to be rude. She just happened to be a rather private person, not used to having guests. Lots of people on our mountain were like that. So I thought little more about it for a while.

When I got around to calling the sheriff's department the next day I was able to reach one of the two deputies I'd met at the lake. Often they would refer you back to the department spokesperson, but this time I got lucky. The investigating deputy wanted to talk.

"We found the missing part in the lake, so we can now determine that it was a young woman who died," he told me. I assumed that he meant that the missing head of the corpse had been found.

I asked him whether they could make a positive ID.

"We know a lot more now than we did before," he replied, "but we still have to wait on dental records. That'll take some time. She lost a lot of teeth. Also, we can say that the body had been drained."

"What do you mean?" I asked.

"Very little blood left in the body," he explained, "so we are beginning to think that the blood had been drained from the body."

"Could it be that she just bled out?" I asked. "Maybe she'd just lost a lot of blood. Then, too, she was in the lake for some time."

"Maybe," the deputy said. "Don't print anything about that just now. We don't know for sure. It looks now that she'd been beaten savagely, then hacked up. You'd lose some blood that way, certainly. A lot of bleeding, sure. For now we only know that she was apparently beaten by blunt force and mutilated."

That word again, I thought. Mutilated.

"Like the birds at the school," I said.

"Yes. Maybe the same perpetrator. Similarities. Let's hold up on any speculation, though, okay? Don't get people too alarmed up there. I'll let you know the details just as soon as things become clear. We're waiting on reports. Wait for the whole story. You can call me in a couple of days."

Nobody would get the story before me was what he was saying. And he'd been generous with what he knew, so I put a lid on the speculative points he'd given me; I wanted to repay his trust with some cooperation. I told him about Laura and what little I knew of her and her sister, Diane. I gave him Laura's Portland phone number and a description of how to find the chapel in the woods.

Maybe there was nothing there, but maybe it would all add up to something in the end. I was no detective. These were just fragments about people I'd met on the mountain, but perhaps it would help him solve the mystery of the murder in the lake and the mutilations.

Murder. There, I'd said it. We'd had a murder in our little mountain community—a brutal, mysterious mutilation. And that didn't make me feel comfortable, keeping what I knew of it bottled up inside my head. Often I would type out matters that were troubling me, which proved to be a very therapeutic thing to do. I was anxious to do that in this case so that I could get it out of my system. The only problem was I didn't have much to type up.

There was something I *could* do in the meantime, though. I thought about mentioning Laura's missing sister in a sidebar news story, just in case it resonated with somebody who might be able to help locate her and solve at least one mystery, even if it was unrelated. I could report, in this sidebar, that Laura's sister had stopped briefly at the chapel in the woods. However, it then occurred to me that the old ladies of the chapel in Sleepy Hollow would dislike any printed reference to them, and that made me a wee bit nervous.

When you feel that you may have bothered people too much in a rural community such as ours, the prudent thing to do is back off for a while. So instead of visiting the chapel in the woods, I sent somebody else from the newspaper staff. They came back with only a photo of the rustic cabin and no comments from the ladies there.

Later in the week, after the autopsy and lab reports on the corpse had come in, I received some clarification from the deputy. The victim was a twenty-five-year-old woman from Portland named Diane Boslar. She had died from blunt blows, which had caused severe trauma. Her body had been dismembered after death and drained of most of its blood. The report also noted that she had floated dead in the lake for more than a week, and possibly two.

I called Laura. She wasn't answering her phone or returning messages. I figured the sheriff's department had already spoken to her in detail and that she now knew probably as much as I did. I kept calling, but she didn't pick up the phone.

The deputies had no immediate suspects that they could identify, but I knew they were up on the mountain making inquiries because a lot of people had seen them in the area. I wondered what the dear old ladies in the woodsy chapel thought of their visits. I assumed the deputies questioned them, even if they seemed harmless.

The one part of the story that I wanted to pursue was an interview with Diane's sister, who ignored my calls. The fact that Laura had claimed that her sister had called her and cried out for help stuck in my mind. However, the deputies had recently confirmed that Diane had been dead about a week prior to Diane's urgent phone call.

Was this a call from beyond the grave? Had Laura spoken to a ghost? It wouldn't be the first time someone claimed to have received a phone call from a dead person. I'd heard about people receiving spirit communications, and it had even happened to me (as I've described earlier in the book).

Now I was beginning to think about Helen. Had she ever dealt with ghostly phone calls? What would she think about this situation? What would she do?

I thought about contacting her but then wondered how and if she could really help me. Besides, there was too much going on locally for me to take a trip to Orcas Island right now, or even to *think* about calling her. We were on the verge of a big news story, and my solid relationship with the deputy sheriff gave me a golden opportunity to break the story first—as long as I kept in daily contact with the local investigation.

The newspaper began to get community backlash from the lack of answers to the mysterious murder at the lake, although people had already forgotten about the bird mutilations, it seemed. After all, that looked like some schoolyard prank that delinquents might play when they had too much summertime on their hands. And those victims were simply a handful of wild birds. The dead girl in the lake was a matter of greater concern. She could be anyone's daughter, sister, or wife. Mountain people disliked people messing with their families or their property.

So we started getting angry calls and letters to the editor indicating the general unrest that was bubbling underneath the surface of our community.

As the days of investigation wore on, it seemed apparent that the deputies still—despite their efforts—were not finding any new leads. So they hammered away at what little they had to work with, going over the same ground and talking to the same people. That seemed to include Laura, and it apparently also included the old ladies in the candle-lit chapel in the woods. I'm certain that Laura told the deputies all about her sister's visit there, just as she had relayed the story to me.

That must have proved frustrating, however, because both Laura and the ladies at the chapel didn't seem to have anything to add to what they'd already said. Additionally, Laura had enough to deal with, given that she had to make funeral arrangements and notify family and friends of her sister's untimely death.

At the newspaper we stayed out of the investigation, content to wait for reliable information from the sheriff's department, which we could print. In subsequent issues of the paper we published simple updates stating that the authorities were continuing to investigate the death of the girl in the lake and would release new information from their probe any day now.

As the buzz died down a little from a lack of new information, I thought about the fact that I had been exposed to a second other-worldly situation subsequent to having learned ghost-hunting techniques from Helen. Certainly I felt no pride in my failure to properly confront, contact, and effectively communicate with a ghostly presence in either instance. However, I decided to cut myself some slack. Okay, I told myself, the big Portland church might not have been actually haunted, as had been reported to me. I mean, I had looked for a ghost in every corner of that huge building and failed to find a thing. I took a small measure of satisfaction from the fact that I had at least salted and staked the grounds.

More recently I had come across the ghost of a dead girl who had called her sister on the phone. Admittedly, I hadn't had any direct contact with this ghostly spirit, but I had also done nothing to try and make contact with it either.

I could take scant comfort from the fact that Laura may have received a phone call from beyond the grave. Perhaps Laura was mistaken regarding the timing of her sister's call. She'd been pretty upset when I'd seen her, and maybe, given her disturbed mental state, she'd been in a state of confusion in general. I could even make the case that the caller had *not* been Laura's sister, although I really found it impossible to believe that Laura couldn't recognize the cries of a blood relative who called out her name.

In the end, after much contemplation, I believed Laura. I believed her when she said that her dead sister had called her.

The lady from the chapel in the woods was not seen again on the main street of our small town. I mused that she may have been more than a little bit mad that I had fingered her and her chapel in the woods by calling them out to the investigating deputies. And perhaps it was misleading of me to have suggested that the good ladies at the chapel might know something about Diane's disappearance. After all, it was only conjecture based on Laura's understanding, whether correct or not, that her sister had visited them before disappearing. And, although they had seemed a bit mysterious in their vague recollection of a young girl named Diane, that didn't make them guilty. Nor did it implicate them in any wrongdoing. They were very private people—older women living alone in the woods—who simply kept to themselves.

As the buzz wore down and the news pace slowed again in the late summertime, I took a couple nights off to relax. One of my favorite ways to unwind and feel a little inner peace was to lie on my back on my living room carpet and just stare up at the night sky through two overhead skylights. The first night I tried this I was able to relax significantly.

That tranquillity was shattered on the second night, however, when

I looked up through the skylight and saw faces staring right back at me. Horrible faces. I was too frightened to stare back at them and quickly left the room. Then my rational mind kicked in. How, it reasoned, could faces appear in the overhead skylight, hovering in the darkness on a peaked roof? Nobody could even stand up there, I told myself. And faces just don't float in the air like disembodied heads, either.

So I walked around the house until I felt calm again and then looked up at the skylights one more time.

The phantom images were still in the window!

Their eyes were terrifying and their gaze transfixed. Who were they, and what were they doing up there?

I tried to look more closely at each face, as frightening as that was for me, and it was then that I seemed to note something familiar in one of the faces in their midst. It looked somewhat like the face of the older lady with the silver hair from the chapel in the woods. Maybe the events of the past few days have left me kind of crazy, I reasoned as I forced myself to look away from the gaze of all of those eyes glaring down at me. They weren't kind or friendly eyes; they were angry eyes.

As quickly as I had turned away, I looked back up at the skylights. Yes, they were still there. And there was no mistaking that they were focused directly on me!

Now, I thought, this is surely a haunting. But was it really? If the woman and her cohorts in the skylight resembled any of the locals I had met on the mountain or in town, then given that these people were all alive, the figures in the skylight couldn't be ghosts. The old woman from the chapel in the woods wasn't a ghost. She was very much a living person and not a deceased spirit.

A thought then crossed my mind—probably out of a scared sense of paranoia from being too close to the murder story and the mutilations. What if these spirits actually knew me? Why else would they visit me personally and stare down at me in this frightening manner? Were these people from the woods? Were they from the chapel?

I felt the overwhelming urge to call Helen on Orcas Island to discuss what I was experiencing. I also wanted to talk to her about the ghost that had called Laura on the phone. She and I had discussed nothing like this in my orientation on de-ghosting houses, unless I had missed something.

Once I got the Outlook Inn's phone number from information, I rang the inn. It rang and rang. With the difference in time zones, I was catching the inn during the dinner rush, which is always big during the late-summer tourist season. The phone continued to ring until finally the unanswered phone call went directly to voicemail. I waited a few minutes and tried calling again. Finally, I got through.

No, I was told, Helen was not at the inn. There was no Helen there. The person on the phone didn't know where she'd gone, but apparently she was no longer in the inn's employ.

Crestfallen, I wondered who else I might consult. I was stuck halfway up a mountain with a bunch of crazies and nobody I could talk to about it. I felt a sinking feeling from the isolation I was experiencing. This was far worse than any fear that the crazy faces in the skylight projected onto me. It was a deep feeling of hopelessness. My home had been invaded, and it was the kind of invasion I could never report to the police. People would just think I was nuts, seeing such unusual things in the skylight. A community journalist doesn't want to be perceived as unstable.

So I went to bed and tried to pretend that the strange events of the evening had never actually happened.

The only problem with that approach was that the same thing happened again the next night. And then a visitor to the house told me he had seen some faces looking down at him from outside the living room. I tried to play all of this down, but I knew I had a real problem on my hands—one that wouldn't go away on its own.

A couple days later I got out of bed and received another scare. Things had been removed from my clothes drawers and dumped on the floor. Meanwhile, things that had been on the floor in my bedroom were now in the clothes drawers. Despite the disarray, all of my clothes drawers were neatly shut. What a mind-blowing trick! I thought. All of this senseless rearranging had been done throughout my bedroom as I had been sleeping nearby. I had heard nothing. All of the outside doors were locked and there was no indication how anyone might have gotten into the room to cause all of the mischief.

It seemed obvious to me that somebody wanted to really upset my world, and they were doing a bang-up job of it. I felt totally vulnerable and violated in my own home. And still, I was unable to tell anybody about any of it: I would sound like a crazy person!

Unfortunately, I was too shaken up by these events to be much good at the newspaper, so I told my staff that I needed to get away for two or three days. I called the Outlook Inn and asked whether Louis was there. He was in Hawaii but would be back the next day. I left word for him that I was coming to visit and to expect me to drop by with a few important questions for him.

I found my way to Sea-Tac Airport and a bus that would take me as far as Anacortes. The bus route did not extend all the way to the state ferry terminal on Fidalgo Island, but I did find an Anacortes taxi service—the only one on the island—that would run me down to the ferry dock.

There I waited for more than two hours for the next ferry to Orcas Island.

After brief stops to disembark cars and passengers at Shaw and Lopez Islands and to take on new westbound traffic, our ferry landed at the Orcas Island ferry terminal. The terminal was miles from Eastsound, where the inn was located. The road to the inn ran up a steep incline and because there were no taxis or buses on the small island, I started walking. I hoped that somebody might take pity on me and stop to offer me a ride. Sure enough, it wasn't long before a yellow International Scout filled with kids and a dog stopped for me.

By the time we got to the village of Eastsound, it had started to rain softly. The Scout pulled up in front of the inn, and I got out and thanked the driver. Walking up to the inn's front door I noticed that the place had been recently painted and the building was undergoing renovation.

At the front desk I asked to see Louis and was advised to take a seat in the dining room. It was midmorning, and there was no wait staff in the dining room so I just sat quietly, watching rain drip down the front windows as I waited for Louis. When he came out of the kitchen and sat next to me, I was pleased to see that he'd lost weight and looked much healthier.

He got right to the point.

"Welcome back!" he said. "I understand you have a question or two for me?"

I didn't hesitate either, but spoke right up. "Last time I was here I spoke with your secretary, Helen, about ghosts and how to make contact with them and then remove them from their haunts. They tell me that Helen is no longer working with you?"

He nodded and smiled and then told me she had moved away from the area.

"Well, I've encountered a few ghostly spirits on my own since moving back to Oregon. I'm on Mount Hood now. Can you help me?" I asked Louis. "I haven't had any success with de-ghosting haunted places, as Helen called it. Maybe I don't have her sensitivity to the spirit world. But I'm worried now about something that's recently happened. I'm being haunted by spirits of living people."

I explained the events in some detail, but Louis didn't seem too concerned.

When I had finished, he said, "All I can tell you is how to protect yourself."

I reiterated how the woman from the chapel in the woods was reputed to have protected herself by purple lights that enveloped her body as she walked through town. I confessed that although I hadn't seen that myself, it did sound impressive.

Louis explained that she might have been wrapped in energy. Clearly, this was his world, and he understood all of these things much better than this country journalist did.

When I asked him how I could protect *myself,* he asked what my objective was. I assured him that I had no intention of striking back or doing anything physical against any of these people . . . or whatever they were. I just wanted them to stop harassing me and stop invading my home. I had no idea how to make a bunch of scary heads floating above my roof disappear.

"This is powerful energy, dark psychic energy at work, as you've described it," he explained. "But you have something stronger. You can repel them and their dark energy with a single thought. Love is stronger than hate. Just think of them and send love back to them."

I told him that sounded like a weak response.

"Oh, no!" he insisted. "See them clearly and then project loving, energetic thoughts toward them. They'll be forced to deal with this energy you send. It'll snap back on them like a rubber band."

"My energy will snap back on them?" I asked.

"Your energy and theirs. You project these thoughts of love to them, and that will stop them. Nothing is stronger than love."

"What about karma?" I asked.

"You're responding by sending them love," he reminded me. "What they do with that is a personal matter."

And it was actually that simple, he convinced me. I thanked Louis, as usual, for his sage guidance and returned to Oregon to deal with these matters. On the trip home, however, I began to wonder whether Louis had fully grasped what was actually going on. His direction was all I had, however, and I figured that he understood the spirit world and psychic energy far better than I ever would.

On the first night of my return to my Brightwood home, I lay again on my back under the skylights. When the faces returned I closed my eyes tightly and focused on them in my mind's eye. Then I projected out to them the closest thing to complete pure love that I could imagine. I felt thoughts of love leaving my body and racing through the night sky to the intended recipients.

The next morning at the newspaper office we learned that a spontaneous fire had erupted in the woods near Sleepy Hollow the previous evening. It was a sort of small wooden cabin serving as a church in the woods that had suddenly caught fire. There was no known cause for the blaze. Our volunteer firefighters up the mountain figured that it might have been started by candles.

I had a different theory, one I kept to myself. It was the same chapel that I had visited earlier while looking for the lost girl. It seemed possible that my intentions of love projected toward the structure and caused the fire. I only hoped that the energy from my thoughts hadn't destroyed something good and pure. It hadn't been my intent to *attack* that chapel in the woods. I only wanted to stop the intruders in my home by sending positive energy their way.

I didn't consider my thoughts to be a weapon. How could loving thoughts be a weapon?

In any event, the faces never returned to haunt me in my skylight, and nothing was ever disturbed in my bedroom again. And our sheriff's deputies never found the murderer, and, for lack of new leads, they slowly abandoned their investigation. The case might still be officially open, but to the best of my knowledge, the probe has ended.

And so have the mysterious mutilations.

7

The Herbalist's Haunted Trailer in the Forest

I was so relieved to have my house free of spirits and the drama of the mutilations behind me that I began to enjoy the early onset of fall. My son and I took a lot of walks on the mountain during his summer visitations after my divorce years earlier. We loved to walk the trails in the lovely Mount Hood National Forest and went mushroom hunting up near Rhododendron every spare moment of the weekends and many late afternoons after work. That introduced us to Lone Dove, a Native American herbalist who lived in the forest with her husband and daughter in a trailer they were house-sitting.

As I recall, we had met them while mushroom hunting for the early chanterelles, mushrooms that grew in fairy rings around old-growth trees and their fallen limbs. Typically we ran in to deer that were looking for the same orange mushrooms, but occasionally we'd meet a knowledgeable commercial mushroom picker up there. Lone Dove, or Tracy as people commonly called her, knew a lot about mushrooms and foraging for them. Her daughter, Missy, who at sixteen was the same age as my son, was fond of drawing, and when we met Missy she was very busy drawing mushrooms and wildflowers in a sketchbook.

Tracy took us on herbal walks through the forest in the days ahead. On these walks my son and I learned to identify herbs on sight, as much from Missy's colorful drawings as by having Tracy point them out to us in the wild. I took the instructional herbal walk first, and then my son went through a special course that Tracy designed for him. She even gave him a special certificate of completion when he had concluded his lessons. It was a good thing we became educated about the herbs, because one of the edible herbs growing wild in the forest resembled a poisonous plant of similar design.

It was so peaceful and relaxing to spend time idly ambling on these nature walks and foraging in the woods instead of worrying about murders and spirits. No more spirits! I told myself, but of course it's impossible to control something like that.

Tracy and her daughter showed us how to crush herbs and cook them over a campfire. We did this on the grounds beside their trailer. We learned how to make a sort of herbal mash into something like bread on a stick the Native American way: by braiding mashed herbs around a stick and then holding it over the fire and roasting it as you would a marshmallow.

We learned to make herbal tea out of sweetgrass that grew wild, although I believe my son considered that an acquired taste.

The grounds and trailer where Tracy and her family lived belonged to a man who had asked them to live there as house sitters, since the place had been vacant for some time and was vulnerable to vandalism and neglect. Apparently he'd found it difficult to sell or even rent the single-wide trailer, although it had a washer and dryer and nearly everything else that a small family living in the woods might need.

It was a curious place, however. One of the things I noticed when we visited it was the old tree in front of the trailer's front entry that had been carved with names and dates that went back a number of years.

The names were funny ones, like Frisky and Rover, and I thought they sounded rather like dog names.

Tracy couldn't shed any light on the story behind the tree, however, and thus it remained a mystery.

In back of the trailer were mostly wild berry bushes that grew thick—salmon berries, high-mountain cranberries, and another variety I couldn't identify. If you pushed your way through these berry thickets you could see a small shed behind the trailer. It was filled with jars that held preserves, and the jars had dates on them. The dates went back quite a few years, long before Tracy and her family had moved here. It seemed odd that somebody had bothered to can all of those preserves and then left them behind, neatly stacked in rows on the wooden shelves of the shed.

There were no neighbors for miles around. A private gravel road led from the main road, which had originally been a fire trail, to the trailer nestled in the trees. It seemed to me that Tracy and her husband, Todd, their daughter, Missy, and their dog lived a rather quiet and idyllic life of rustic seclusion cradled in the bosom of nature.

I loved going over to their house to share time around the campfire with them or prepare mushrooms with Tracy and her daughter. Todd pretty much stayed to himself and was often gone. So it was frequently just the four of us—Tracy, Missy, my son, and me—who cooked up the herbs we had gathered that day or prepared a big kettle of fresh mushrooms on the stove inside.

I always thought that the family's home in the woods was perfect for them, but after I'd known Tracy and Todd for some time, they started to tell me about some odd things that happened there at night, including odd noises that they couldn't account for. I had lived in a trailer myself, near Skyline Marina when I worked in Anacortes, and the wind would blow parts of my aluminum house across the bluff. As a result, I knew firsthand how flimsy and creaky trailers could be. After all, they're tin boxes designed for living on the fly. So I dismissed Todd and Tracy's comments about strange noises in the house. All buildings creak and groan from time to time as they settle, and mobile homes were simply flimsier and more vulnerable to every gust of wind that might blow their way.

Only there was very little wind in the woods, given that the mobile home was surrounded by huge old-growth trees. Still, they could get some serious weather up there on Mount Hood. Maybe temperature fluctuations or moisture were the cause of the creaking in the old trailer house.

Frankly, I probably wouldn't have given their casual remarks about oddities in the trailer much thought if it hadn't been for something that Missy shared with me. She told me an elaborate story about a little girl with curly blond hair who visited her at night. Missy said the girl would visit frequently and without warning. That wasn't the problem, though. The problem, according to Missy, was that the girl didn't seem to like her parents. I believed that this blond-haired girl was no doubt an imaginary playmate of Missy's, and I speculated that Missy was projecting her own dislike of her parents onto the purported views of this imaginary friend.

There were two very different versions of the girl with the golden curls who played with Missy. Todd and Tracy told me that their teenage daughter was lonely and had invented the visitor in her mind. Indeed, there were no playmates for Missy for miles around, and she didn't attend school. Furthermore, the family seldom went into town. Missy was all alone, except for Todd and Tracy, and, like most teenagers, no doubt she had issues with her parents.

Missy's version of the story was that the girl was very real, even if she couldn't be seen in a physical sense. Missy claimed that she could see her in her mind and knew she was there for her. She claimed that the two of them played alone on Missy's bed for hours. When her parents would tell Missy to stop playing and go to sleep, the girl with the golden curls would become angry with them and attack them.

The only part of the two stories that seemed consistent was that Todd and Tracy apparently *were* attacked at night as they slept. They described the attacks as feeling as though some invisible force had entered their bed and was trying to strangle them. Given this, they were a little afraid to sleep in their own bed at night.

Missy, on the other hand, was delighted to have such a supportive playmate who dropped in out of nowhere to spend time with her.

In any event, I listened to all of the stories but didn't really get involved in the discussion. They were my friends, and I enjoyed their company and so we went along like that for some time, with my son and me visiting them and continuing our herbal walks and cooking herbs over an open campfire outside their mobile home. Their dog was always close at hand, happy to be part of the activities. I never saw it on a leash or a tether, and I never saw it leave the property unless it was with us.

Pretty soon I realized that although my friends were comfortable living in that trailer in the woods, they were nonetheless on edge and not happy whenever night fell upon them and things seemed to get a bit strange inside their metal box. It didn't matter that they might have been merely imagining strange things going on. Tracy and Todd had real trouble sleeping and seemed to be getting somewhat paranoid about things.

I felt sorry for them and offered to help in any way I could. Tracy suggested that I should intercede by getting to the bottom of things. Specifically, they wanted me to talk with their daughter, because Missy seemed to find it easy to speak with me. Tracy and Todd encouraged me to look at the situation and determine whether Missy really thought that she saw a little girl with blond curls, or whether she was just making the whole thing up.

Because Missy had gone on herbal walks to find mushrooms with us and also was a friend to my son, I had likewise never found it difficult to speak with her. So I agreed to talk to her. I can mediate this little problem, I thought to myself. These people just have trouble talking to each other and harbor some deeply held resentment that no doubt can be quickly cleared up.

Tracy's daughter slept on a bed in a corner of the living room that opened directly to the kitchen, with the outside door just across the room and opposite the bed. It was a small area, and Missy shared it with a lot of people if they happened to be in the front room or kitchen, or even if they were merely entering or exiting the trailer. Next to Missy's bed was a cardboard filing cabinet with four drawers stuffed full of her clothes. Two walls of the room held several colorful sketches of plants, flowers, and unicorns that the teenager had drawn.

When I told Missy that I wanted to have a chat with her, she seemed happy to speak with me. I spoke with her alone in the trailer, sitting on her bed. She wanted to tell me all about the girl with the golden curls and was busy sketching a picture of her while we spoke. Had she drawn the girl to look like herself? I wondered. No, the girl with the blond curls didn't resemble Missy at all. Instead, she looked to be approximately eight or nine years old, younger and smaller than Missy. Missy has quite a vivid and detailed imagination, I thought to myself as I looked at the sketch.

Missy admitted to me that the little blond girl who visited her in the trailer couldn't be seen in the normal sense. However, she insisted that this playmate was with her much of the time and that she could see her. Moreover, she maintained that I could see her too, if I really wanted to.

Missy stood up to show me her friend's height. The younger girl was approximately four feet tall. Missy's picture of her revealed faint freckles, and she was smiling, but her eyes were unusual in that they stared right back at me in a slightly sad sort of way, making her look old beyond her years. Missy told me that her small friend had a ready smile, but only for her special friend. She didn't seem to like other people—at least, she didn't like Tracy and Todd. I tried to corner

Missy on this point, because it really sounded as though her imaginary friend was speaking more for Missy than for herself and that it was really Missy who was unhappy with her parents.

No. Missy insisted that this was coming directly from the little girl.

She wouldn't tell me her name, however, and then went on to tell me that the girl had told Missy her name but had made her swear not to tell it to anyone. This seemed dubious to me, and once again seemed to indicate that the girl was really just an extension of Missy herself. I asked whether the girl wanted to remain completely anonymous, and whether it was okay that Missy had told me about her. Missy said neither issue was a problem. The girl wasn't afraid of anyone or anything. She wanted Missy to know that and to know that she would protect her.

I asked Missy whether she felt that she really needed protection, and she replied that she didn't, but added that her friend was very protective of her just the same. Then Missy began to tell me about some games that she played with the blond girl. The girl would ask her to identify things in the woods near the trailer or identify objects that were stored in the old shed in the back. She would talk about the trees and ask Missy to guess which ones were the oldest.

According to my teenage friend, her blond playmate seemed to know a lot of history about the area. Apparently she talked about people who'd lived there. She said that she hadn't liked most of them; she had bad things to say about them. On the other hand, she spoke lovingly of the children who'd lived there, particularly the young girls she'd befriended. She said they were her special friends and she protected them.

I asked Missy for details about the other people who had lived there and whether she knew anything about the relationship the little girl once had with them. But Missy couldn't convey more information about this, nor had she asked her friend for any details. Missy said she just listened to what the girl told her, because the girl had a lot to say. Apparently Missy never asked her much in return.

Also, it was all Missy could do to listen, because she said she had to concentrate very hard to understand the girl. I asked how the girl sounded when she spoke, and Missy reported that the girl's speech wasn't audible to anyone but her—that she heard it all inside her head. That's why she had to concentrate so hard to hear her, she told me.

The girl told Missy that many families had brought dogs to the trailer to live with them, but that they were all bad dogs that barked too much and got the children in trouble. The dogs were a bother, she told Missy. Strangely, the girl with the blond curls knew all of their names. She would recite these names and describe the dogs to Missy. I asked Missy how many dogs we were talking about, but she only remembered that the little girl had recited many names. When pressed, however, Missy could tell me a couple of them: Frisky, Duke, and Rover. Apparently none of the dogs had lived too long, according to the girl.

At this point in our conversation about her playmate, Missy said that I could meet her myself and that I should be able to see her too. She also insisted that I would be able to hear her friend.

"You'll see," Missy told me. "Just try it. She might really like you."

It seemed unlikely to me that I would be able to see or hear the girl, and I told Missy that the girl was her special playmate and that nobody else could probably see her.

I decided that I needed to speak to Tracy and Todd in more depth about this situation in order to get a better perspective on what was really going on here. After I had finished chatting with Missy, I went outside to find them. Tracy was drying herbs by the campfire, and Todd was sitting in the car listening to the radio. There wasn't much privacy in the trailer, so they'd remained outside while I spoke to their daughter.

After Tracy and I convinced Todd to join us on the porch, I gave them a quick rundown of what Missy had told me about her playmate with the golden curls. Then I told them that I wanted to get their perspective on things to see if I could help. I wanted details.

Todd in particular seemed eager to talk.

"It's gotten to where I almost don't want to go in there to sleep at night," he said, pointing to the back of the trailer. He and Tracy had a bedroom at the trailer's far end, through the living room and kitchen and down a long hallway in the center that included a laundry area. It was the only real bedroom in the small mobile home.

I pressed him to explain.

"Well," he said, "I'll be in bed, trying to tell myself that everything's fine. Things will get real quiet—almost too quiet. I'll start to fall asleep, and then in the middle of getting some real rest, I feel something around my neck—like somebody's trying to strangle me!"

"Choking you with their hands?" I asked.

"That's what it feels like," Todd said. "Hands wrapped around my neck and squeezing me tight."

"Did you ever see anything when this happened?" I asked him.

"No, nothing," Todd said. "It's dark, but I can tell somebody's there. I see Tracy beside me sleeping. Nothing's bothering *her*!"

I asked him if this had happened more than once.

"Many times," he replied. "I don't know how many times, but more than a couple, for sure. And I don't know what it could be, but it's spooky, let me tell you. I've never had anything like this happen to me before."

I asked him how long it had been going on and whether it had happened before they moved to the trailer in the forest.

"No," he said, "never before we came here. We've been here— what?—six months now? Six months. It started happening a few weeks after we moved in."

I asked him if the choking seemed personally directed at him like an attack, or if he might possibly be choking on his own during his sleep. He told me that he normally had no trouble sleeping and insisted he had no health condition that might cause him to choke on his own in this way.

"It's like someone is trying to get me, really trying to kill me," Todd said, "someone or something."

Not ready to accept the invisible force theory, I began to ask Todd a series of questions about his emotional state, treading very carefully. He said that he had never been treated or diagnosed for anything resembling a mental problem or nerves and that he was not a skittish sort of person.

So I asked whether he had been drinking before retiring on any of the nights when the choking sensation occurred.

Again, he insisted that he'd been absolutely sober and sane.

I asked whether he got along well with Missy. His answer surprised me somewhat.

"I'm not her natural father," he told me. "She's Tracy's girl. But I've known her since she was a baby. I even changed her diapers. We've crossed the country together and lived together in a car."

Again, I asked whether there was any tension between him and Missy.

"She's a teenager," was all Todd would say. "We have our little problems, sure. I tell her how things are and what to do, and she doesn't always like that. She sometimes acts like she doesn't think much of me, but we all get along okay for the most part. Don't we?" he asked, turning to Tracy.

Tracy looked down at the porch, then up at Todd. She said nothing, preferring to communicate with him silently in that nonverbal way that spouses often do.

"Well, did Missy ever throw anything at you or yell at you?" I asked Todd.

"Nah," he said. "I wouldn't let her. We're okay. Let's just say she doesn't like me as much as she likes her mom, maybe. But that's natural, I guess."

I asked him if he and Missy ever did things together in order to bond as father and daughter.

He reminded me that Missy wasn't his own daughter and told me that she had accompanied him to work just the other week when he had been employed as a night watchman in town for a while.

I asked if they had worked well together, to which Todd replied that Missy hadn't actually worked with him but had merely gone along to keep him company.

"Did she *want* to go with you?" I asked.

"I guess," he said. "She made some coffee and brought it along."

I turned to Tracy. "How about you?" I asked her. "You ever feel like somebody's trying to choke you at night?"

She shook her head.

"Ever feel like something strange is in the room when you're in bed?"

She took her time before answering. "Well," she replied, "not exactly. Once, maybe, I felt like something was touching me, but I woke up right away. And it was nothing."

I asked her to describe what it had been like in the room when that happened.

She said she had been lying with Todd in the bed.

I pressed her to describe how the room felt to her.

"It was a little cold, maybe," Tracy said. "But it wasn't all that warm that night, anyway."

"Did you feel a sudden chill in the room that came upon you and then seemed to disappear?" I asked.

"Yeah," she said. "It didn't last long. Most likely, I was just scared a bit."

"Scared of what?" I pressed.

"Oh, I don't know," she said. "I just felt funny there for a minute. But it was nothing."

I asked her if she thought her house might be haunted.

She looked at me a long time before answering. "Maybe we should check that out," she told me. "Maybe it *is* haunted. I don't know. Maybe there's a reason this trailer sat vacant for so long, and nobody wanted to stay here."

I told her that I'd been trained by someone who had a lot of experience dealing with haunted houses.

"So why don't you check this out for us?" she said to me. "Is there some way you can do that?"

I told her I would try but added that I hadn't had any previous success finding and eliminating ghosts.

We agreed that I should come back the next night, just before the family normally went to bed. Todd and Tracy told me that they'd be happy to clear out of their home while I checked things out for them inside the trailer.

Given my track record since learning the tricks of the trade from Helen, I had faint confidence that I could help them. I had failed to make contact with or even locate a ghost on my two previous attempts. Three strikes and you're out, I told myself. If I failed this time, perhaps I would give the whole thing up.

I felt that I had to try to help my friends, however. They were so alone and vulnerable in that mobile home at the end of the gravel drive, surrounded by the darkness of thick-growth forest.

When I went back inside to say good-bye to Missy, she was still sitting on her bed, drawing. She jumped up with enthusiasm to show me her new sketch. It was another picture of the girl with the golden curls.

"This is more the way she usually looks!" Missy told me. It did look slightly different from the earlier depiction. The girl still looked about eight or nine, and she still had blond hair, but her eyes looked darker than in the drawing I'd seen earlier.

"Did you talk to my mom and Todd about her?" she asked.

I told her I had.

"She doesn't like them," Missy reiterated. "She wants them out of here."

I picked up Missy's latest drawing and looked at it more closely. It looked just like a little girl.

On my way back to my car I walked past Tracy's drying herbs and the campfire. I started walking back to the elderberry trees that hung over my car where the gravel road ended. Something caught my eye, and I stopped. It was the old tree with the carved names on the trunk. I'd passed it many times before, but something clicked in my head at this moment as I glanced at the names in the tree. Some had been there for some time and were barely legible now.

"Frisky—May 30," the first carving read.

"Rover—July 22," the next carving read.

All of a sudden I realized something. A sick feeling in my gut told me that these were the names of dogs who had lived there and a record of the day that each one had died.

8

Confronting the Spirit in the Trailer

Driving away from Tracy's trailer in the forest I felt that I had to do whatever I could to help my friends remove whatever was inhabiting their home. There simply was no feeling of peace and safety there when the sun went down. I was assuming, therefore, that whatever was befriending the girl and bothering her parents was not a figment of anyone's imagination or a result of family infighting, but rather some outside force. If wrong, at least I would be trying to resolve the situation for them by checking things out and attempting to remove the problem.

The intruder appeared to be a malevolent ghost who identified positively with the daughter but attacked Tracy and Todd. Thinking back to my training with Helen, it also seemed possible that the spirit might be one of those energy bodies that are formed and fed by people's negative thoughts. In that case I would find no ghost in the traditional sense and would simply need to explain the situation to Tracy, Todd, and Missy so that they could attempt to dissolve the energy body themselves. Their other option would be for them to move out of the trailer. It seemed that others had moved away from the trailer in

113

a hurry, judging by the preserves that had been left perfectly intact in rows inside the back shed.

Whatever was going on, I really hoped I could achieve some concrete success in removing the disruptive energy from the house.

At home, I assembled my ghost-hunting kit with the tools Helen had encouraged me to use, should I encounter a ghost who refused to leave peacefully. I hoped I wouldn't need any of them, however, to convince an unwanted spirit to vacate the trailer.

I mentally rehearsed the exorcism and how it might go. My Brightwood home seemed so peaceful now that the floating heads were gone and the sister of the missing girl had left our community. I hoped that Tracy's home in the forest would be just as peaceful when I finished my task the following night. I visualized how I might go about making contact and communicating with the spirit in the trailer. Missy felt that the girl with the golden curls would open up to me freely, should I encounter her. I had no expectation that things would go easily, but I did expect that contact with and extraction of this ghost would be possible. I would simply connect with the little girl psychically and ask her to leave.

The next evening, on the drive over to the mobile home, I fluctuated between feeling confident that I had been properly trained to a nagging fear that I wouldn't be able to communicate without words with a spirit that plainly disliked adults. I clung to the hope that I would find nothing there. Maybe I could simply establish that the family members couldn't get along with one another and that they were engaged in psychic warfare and their own petty mind games. Wrestling with all of this uncertainty on my drive over to the trailer, I finally managed to tune out my concerns for a while, thinking only of what steps I would take to make contact with whatever might greet me in the dark.

When I pulled up the driveway, the entire family, including their sweet dog, sat on the front steps of the trailer in the pleasant warmth of the evening. There were no sounds in the woods. It was a quiet night. I found it hard to believe how still everything was. There weren't even any mosquitoes buzzing about.

The family stepped aside to allow me to enter the trailer, but as I started up the wooden steps, Tracy held up a hand to stop me.

"Are you sure you want to do this?" she asked. "You don't have to, you know. It's up to you, totally."

I smiled faintly. "No problem," I replied.

"But what if it doesn't work?" Todd asked.

"Don't worry," I said. "I have backup plans. All will be well."

Missy looked concerned.

"Just don't make her mad, okay?" she told me. "She's a nice little girl—really. Just talk to her softly and don't make her mad. I think she'll talk to you. Show her my drawings and tell her how you talked with me about her. Tell her you're my friend. Then she might like you."

"Sounds good," I said. "Where's your sketch pad right now?"

"It's on my bed, in the corner by the wall," she said. "She'll meet you there if you call for her."

I told the family to stay outside for a few minutes and not to worry. Then I walked into the trailer with my bag of tricks and closed the door behind me.

It was dark inside and absolutely still. I felt a great uneasiness all around me, which I assumed was probably just my own nervousness. I reached around the door and flicked on the overhead light, but it provided little lighting for the small room.

Without looking around, I walked directly to Missy's half-made bed and reached across it for the sketchbook in its corner. I sat down and opened the book, flipping through the pages until I located a colorful drawing of the golden-haired girl.

I studied the picture for a moment or two until I felt that I had a good feeling for how the girl looked to Missy. The picture was, after all, an impression of the way Missy saw her in her mind's eye. I cleared my mind and then visualized a clean black slate with the picture of the girl mounted on it staring straight back at me. I visualized seeing the girl and manifesting her in the room with me. Without words, I called out for her to come to me.

When it was time to open my eyes again, I was understandably afraid to do so. What if she was standing there? Was I really prepared for her?

At last I summoned enough courage to open my eyes. Nothing. I was still alone in the trailer, it seemed to me, and things were deathly quiet.

I decided to speak to the girl out loud.

"Hello," I said. "I know you're here. I can't see you yet, but I know you can see me and that you're here. Missy sent me. I'm Missy's friend. She told me all about you and showed me pictures of you. So I know who you are."

Nothing.

"It's okay," I said. "You can come out now and sit with me here on the bed, as you did with Missy. I'm Missy's friend. I want to be your friend too."

Still nothing.

I got very quiet inside of myself with my feet firmly grounded on the floor and my hands extended wide at my sides. I cleared my mind and sat on the edge of the bed with perfectly erect posture, attempting to get into a more meditative state of mind. I visualized a clear blank slate in my mind's eye again and then waited to see an actual image or impression of this ghostly spirit. If I did this correctly, it would be like looking through special binoculars at someone standing near me— something hard to detect with my eyes alone.

Where was this ghostly spirit? Would she appear to me?

Again I tried visualizing how the little girl appeared in Missy's depictions of her, and again I tried pasting that two-dimensional representation on the blank screen of my mind's eye. But again there was nothing.

So I tried clearing the slate and just listened keenly. The trailer was very still. I was unable to hear crickets or normal forest sounds outside.

With a flash of inspiration, I stood up quickly and started strolling through the narrow elongated mobile home, unhooking the wooden gate that separated the living room from the hallway leading to the back of the trailer. It seemed curious, I thought, that they used a child-proof gate to separate the hallway and backroom from the main entry space. I doubted that the gate proved to be any barrier to the girl with the blond curls.

The hallway had a washer and dryer on one side, which I squeezed by. At the end of the otherwise bare hallway, at the very back end of the single-wide trailer, was Tracy and Todd's bedroom.

I moved slowly around their room without hearing, seeing, or sensing anything. I flicked off the light after circling the room and returned down the hallway.

Back in the main entry I sat on Missy's bed in the corner again, going deeper and deeper into a super-consciousness level of awareness where I might pick up some subtle activity. But again nothing happened. It was a bit embarrassing on a personal level to consider that I was failing to make contact with a ghost that everyone who lived here seemed to know intimately. This nonevent was beginning to look exactly like my pathetic effort inside the big Portland church.

I believed it to be exactly this time of day that the spirit who haunted the trailer would typically make itself known to the family. Missy would be coming indoors, and her parents would be starting to think about retiring. But then I second-guessed myself. Maybe it was still too early in the evening for the ghost to appear.

It occurred to me that perhaps it needed to be dark inside the trailer. I walked over to the light switch and turned off the light in the front end of the trailer. With no light down the hallway and the heavy forest canopy that shrouded the trailer in a total blackout, I was unable to see even my hand at this point.

Enough, I thought.

I opened the door and stepped outside. The family was sitting on the lower steps.

"Anybody got a flashlight?" I asked them.

Todd stood up. "Got one in the car," he said. "Be right back."

He returned with one of those long black flashlights that night watchmen usually carry. It had heft and was heavy.

Looking at the family on the porch, I could see worry and anticipation wrinkled on all three of their faces, but I said nothing and slipped back into the trailer, flashlight in hand.

I walked over to the bed, beaming the light ahead of me the whole way. I was focused on that corner of the room and, based on what Missy had told me, I expected to find the girl there. With the light shining on the bed, I opened Missy's sketchbook again and, finding a picture of the girl with the curls, I held the opened book up to the light.

"I have your picture," I said aloud, hoping to attract the ghost girl. "Missy said I could look at your pictures in her book. I'm her friend. Missy told me to come here tonight to meet you. Will you come see me? I want to see you. I want to be your friend."

Self-consciously, I closed the book. I was talking to myself in the dark in an empty trailer and was feeling rather foolish. There seemed to be nobody around but me.

I flicked off the flashlight and just sat there with my head down, thinking that I must be missing something. But what? I sat waiting for inspiration for what seemed like several minutes. I was nearly out of ideas.

I flicked on the flashlight and lifted my head.

As I did so, I scared myself with the expectation that something or someone was very near and almost on top of me.

Without turning my head, my eyes darted from side to side.

Apparently I was scaring myself at this point. I saw nothing.

I stood up and walked to the kitchen sink. I looked at the counters.

I opened all of the drawers. I looked behind the doorway in the corner of the kitchen. Might as well do one final sweep before leaving, to make certain I've checked everything, I decided.

I walked around the kitchen table set near Missy's bed. I looked under the table. I walked to the hallway and unhooked the childproof wooden gate again.

Stepping into the hallway, I pointed the light of the heavy flashlight onto the floor to guide my feet. I was walking a bit faster now, anxious to make one final check through the entire trailer so that I could leave.

When I reached the washer and dryer I almost bumped into them, given that I was looking down at my feet with the light still fixed on the floor.

Looking up, I gasped, with my mouth wide open. There was something sitting on top of the washer! I started to scream but was so frightened that no sound came out of my mouth. Someone was sitting on the washing machine, but it didn't look human. It was a horribly disfigured creature that had dark wrinkled skin and straight gray hair down to its waist. Given its long hair, it looked to be female, but not a girl and not really a woman either. It was something totally different—that much I knew. And it was waiting there in the darkness of the narrow hallway for me, as though it had lured me there and now had trapped me.

It glared at me with dark red eyes that were filled with contempt. The creature seemed incensed that I'd been searching for it and that I'd now invaded its space. Clearly it didn't want me there.

I looked away. When I looked back, I hoped it would be gone. But it was still there, glaring at me with those brooding eyes.

Trying to control myself, I struggled to speak.

"You—you are not a little girl!" I said to it, almost as a weak challenge under my breath. "You're a great deceiver, a dark one. Aren't you?" I challenged it.

In a flash, the hideous creature transformed itself before my eyes into the image of an eight- or nine-year-old girl with long golden curls. Suddenly it had the innocent look of a child at play, looking for a friend.

"You cannot deceive me!" I said a bit louder. "I know what you truly are! Leave here at once! This is not your home!"

The blond child held its gaze, without moving or responding.

"I order you to leave! Be gone now!" I repeated.

Again I looked into that cunning face, knowing that I couldn't remain in that corridor for long.

I began backing slowly out of the hallway then returned to the living room and searched for my gym bag, which lay in there somewhere. When I found it near the bed, I grabbed it and then flicked on the overhead light.

Frantically I rustled through the bag, with my hands shaking. Tricks, tricks, I needed tricks! Realizing that this was decidedly no ghost of a dead little girl, I began to question whether my tools would work. What was that creature in the hallway? A spirit of some sort, I determined, but it didn't look remotely human—either dead or alive. Nor was it likely one of Helen's energy formations—a cloudy body formed by people's negative energy and thoughtforms. This being had a body that was fully formed. It had a head with eyes and ears and a body with arms and some sort of twisted legs.

I looked at my options in the bag. My tools didn't seem adequate, and I felt outmatched. My frantic rummaging through the bag brought some of the spikes to the surface, standing upright in the open bag, ready for action. I left the open gym bag on the floor and reached for the door handle.

With just my head sticking out the door, I called to the family huddled on the bottom steps with their dog. It was a peaceful, pleasant early autumn night outside the trailer where they sat. Inside was a different story. I meant to keep them on the outside tonight.

"Okay," I told them, as calmly as I could. "I've made contact with the spirit in your home. I will now remove it. Don't worry."

"No kidding?" Tracy said. "You gonna be okay in there?"

"I'll be okay," I tried to assure them. Then I looked directly at Missy, who seemed concerned. "Don't worry about your little friend," I told her. "I'm going to help her move along now. She really doesn't belong here, you know. It's time for her to leave. Everything will be fine."

I closed the door and sat down on Missy's bed. I looked again inside the gym bag at its contents, wondering how to proceed and the steps that should be taken. I had the fake holy water, the spikes to seal the grounds at the four cardinal corners, and the kosher salt to draw a line around the building. What I really had were tools of persuasion to ward off ghosts. What was lurking in the trailer, however, didn't appear to be like the ghost of any dead person I'd ever seen.

It was some other spirit—and a very dark one at that.

I was unsure of myself, so I decided to go by the numbers as they'd been outlined for me by Helen. Just follow the procedures, I told myself. Following orders in this robotic manner left less room for uncertainty and helped steady my nerves somewhat.

As I lifted one of the spikes out of the bag, I weighed my options and realized the only tool I could use inside the house was the holy water. My *fake* holy water, that is, given that it had never been properly sanctioned by a priest. Instead, it was water that I'd put outside under the moonlight in a glass jar with a quartz crystal in it. Both the moonlight and the crystal were meant to purify it, which was some small comfort. I'd consumed water made overnight in this manner before and found it to be extremely soft and sweet. I also believed that it had healing properties. Tracy, the herbalist, told me it did. It would be a strange bit of synchronicity if Tracy's magic concoction would now free her of the spirit haunting her house.

I crept my way to the corridor and opened the childproof gate.

There was no light between the front room and the backroom, and I had left the flashlight behind. When my timid steps brought me to the washer and dryer, I saw nothing there. I reached around, figuring the darkness might be hiding something.

But there was nothing.

The vial of water was in my right hand, its contents ready to be thrown at the creature. I scanned the hallway, turning my head in every direction in search of the dark spirit. Had it moved? Not seeing it, I advanced to the end of the narrow hallway and entered the back bedroom, which was equally dark. I rushed to the wall switch and turned on the light. I spun away from the wall, expecting the dark spirit to pounce on me out of nowhere.

When nothing happened, I looked into the closet, under the bed, and behind the curtains. Nothing.

"I know you're here somewhere," I said aloud. "You can't avoid me. I'm not leaving until I remove you from this house."

My voice broke the silence and then fell flat, leaving the room deathly still again.

"Okay," I said. "I'm coming in."

I left the room with the light still burning and worked my way through the narrow corridor again.

Back in the front room I scanned every corner, certain that I must have flushed the spirit to this end of the building and that I had it cornered. But I couldn't fight what I couldn't see.

I sat on the bed, trying to attain an inner stillness so as to sense the spirit's presence somewhere in the room. I figured the only way I could determine its location was to sense it with my awareness.

This spirit could pop in and pop out at any time.

In the next moment I sensed that the room was filled with the spirit's presence and that I had indeed cornered it. And I guessed it wouldn't leave, because it was now playing with me, tormenting me.

The hunter had become the hunted.

How old was this malevolent spirit, and how many people had it tormented right here in this trailer throughout the years?

When I sensed the foul presence of the creature directly in front of me, I uncorked the vial of holy water and tossed its contents straight ahead. The water fell onto a scatter rug in the middle of the front room. Had it done any good? How would I know whether it had?

I sat down on the bed and tried to feel the presence of the spirit again. Yes, it was right here and every bit as strong and foreboding as it had before. But in addition, now I was sensing blind rage. No doubt I was in mortal danger, so I grabbed the gym bag and rushed out the door.

"I'm going to put stakes around the corners of the house to drive out the spirit!" I told the family on the front steps as I hurriedly pushed past them. They moved quickly out of the way and then, together with their dog, they took off down the gravel road, apparently to ride out the storm some distance from the trailer. A big part of me wanted to walk away too.

I placed the first stake in the ground in the southern corner near the place where Tracy dried her herbs. I had included a lightweight hammer in the bag so that I could drive the stakes deep into the earth.

"I banish thee from these grounds!" I said when the first stake was embedded. "You may not enter these grounds again."

I made the same pronouncement when I moved to the eastern corner of the lot, then the north corner, and then the western corner. In addition to driving the stakes into each spot, all four cardinal points had been addressed as watchtowers to guard the property and ward off evil spirits.

Had these efforts made any difference? I put the hammer back in the bag and reentered the trailer. Seeing and hearing nothing, I initially felt relieved. Then, after sitting quietly and centering myself again, I groaned softly. I could still sense the creature's presence in the front room. It hadn't moved at all.

I went back outside to salt the grounds. I began sprinkling it in one continuous line around the property, working again from the southern side to the eastern side and around the northern side to the trailer's western side.

Stay outside this line, away from this property, I said silently to the creature, in my head. Then I decided to drive the point home.

"I have staked the property and salted the grounds to drive you from this house!" I said out loud. "I banish thee! Be gone now from this home! You cannot enter these grounds again!"

Then I just stood there, depleted of salt and completely out of stakes. Were my efforts enough? These measures were supposed to drive ghosts out of buildings, but what effect would they have on a malevolent spirit who was probably *not* a departed human soul?

The family was watching from some distance away, down the gravel road. They waved at me, noting that I had stopped all of my pounding and sprinkling around the building.

I gave them a thumbs-up sign, not wanting to worry them. After all, I had followed the procedures to the letter, as best I understood them.

I then walked up the front steps and opened the door, wondering what I might find.

I had nothing else in me. My battle was over, one way or the other.

There was a mess in the front room where things had been tossed on the floor. It was a chaotic scene and one that I was not prepared to see. Minutes before, the place had been very neat.

It seemed that this malevolent spirit was now angry and probably upset with me and my actions. Apparently it felt that I was the one who should leave at this time. I sat on the floor inside the door, wondering what I might do. I felt completely defeated.

Then I remembered the mirror. I had a mirror in the bag. The principle behind the mirror had something to do with mirror magick, but I hadn't been trained in this practice and didn't know how to use the mirror. It was time to improvise. What did I have to lose? I would throw everything that I had at this thing.

I had with me the largest mirror that I could fit in the gym bag—a mirror I had once used for shaving in my alternate bathroom downstairs. Fortunately, bouncing around with the spikes and hammer hadn't cracked it. I pulled it out of the bag and looked at it.

"I have something for you," I said aloud to the spirit, "and I think you're going to like it. It's a peace offering. I'm sorry that I've upset you. I'm giving you this magick mirror to make up for that."

Although I suggested to the spirit that the mirror was a gift, it was just another tool to remove the spirit. Looking at the mirror, I mulled over the little I had ever heard or read about mirror magick—which was next to nothing. I had once looked into a Rosicrucian study course, and the good people of the Ancient Mystical Order Rosae Crucis (AMORC) had offered me a lesson in mirror magick if I joined their order. But I'd never signed up. I had also read in an Eastern spiritual text how yogis would sometimes look into a mirror to realize their spiritual double and to actualize it. I, however, had never actually tried this practice myself.

Mirrors had always seemed innately magical to me, like some modern residue left over from some ancient alchemical procedure. How mirrors are made is a fascinating process in and of itself: The glass inside the mirror, originally in a liquid state, undergoes a gaseous transformation of some sort and then ultimately becomes solid. When you look into a mirror it reveals you to yourself. It reflects your image or, more precisely, it reflects light bounced off you. The image that you see is not exactly a true representation of how you actually look. Concave or convex bends in a mirror's surface twist the reflected images around, causing hideous distortions of what we consider reality. Although this mirror from my house was neither concave nor convex, everything in it appeared backward.

Even if mirrors aren't magical, they can certainly seem mystical.

The dead have no normal physical form, making it hard to bounce light off them. They spend their afterlife in spirit form as a kind of ethereal energy. I thought how frustrating it must be for them to hang onto an illusion of being present in the physical world.

Would this lack of a normal physical image also be frustrating to other spirits? Would it frustrate a demon?

I really didn't know what I had cornered in that tiny metal trailer, but it did seem to be curious, and it did seem to desire interaction.

I looked into the mirror and saw my own reflection.

"See me in the mirror?" I said to the spirit. "Would you like to see yourself in the mirror too?"

I flicked off the overhead light and sat down near the flashlight. I flicked it on and started waving it in little circles on the floor all around us. Maybe I could lure the spirit into the mirror.

"Follow the light," I said. "It will take you to the mirror, where you can see yourself and be whole."

I continued to tease the spirit with the light, and then shined it directly in front of the mirror. Then I shined the light directly on the mirror itself.

Nothing appeared.

"Now I will put you in the light and you can see your physical form in the mirror," I said. "This is a rare gift that I offer you. Today you will be whole. Today you will have form."

I pointed the mirror toward the area where the presence of the spirit seemed the strongest to me. Oh, yes, it was interested; I could feel it.

I pointed the light over the top of the mirror, which I had propped on the floor. No, that wouldn't work. The light needed to bounce off something and reflect back onto the mirror.

So I propped the mirror against the door and stood back. Then I shined the light from across the room in the general direction of the mirror. I moved about the room, trying to catch different angles to reflect a light image onto the mirror.

"That's it," I advised. "Go into the mirror. Let yourself get lost in the mirror. The mirror gives you form. The mirror makes you whole. Go into the mirror. Enter the mirror."

I sensed a difference in the room. The spirit no longer felt ominous, nor did it feel as if it was near me. It felt as though it was gone.

In a flash I grabbed the mirror, with the flashlight still in one hand. I opened the door and stepped onto the front steps. I closed the door quickly and then dropped the mirror, face up.

Using the big heavy flashlight, I began shattering the glass in the mirror.

"I release you from this house and free you to leave! You're free! You're no longer a part of this house. Leave this place now and do not return! I banish you!"

Strangely, I felt that this bit of trickery had worked. I felt relieved, and I felt as if the spirit was gone, given that I didn't sense it anymore.

I walked slowly down the stairs, wondering if I were truly clear of danger. I walked toward the gravel road at the edge of the grounds. Tracy started to walk out to meet me, followed closely by Todd, Missy, and their dog.

I handed the flashlight to Todd. "Thanks, Todd. The flashlight helped. I think you'll be okay now. I got it out of the house."

Then I turned to Tracy. "Look," I told her, "I'm afraid that I had to break a mirror on the front steps. But don't worry. It was one that I brought. But you'll want to sweep that up before anyone cuts themselves on it. Also, the front room is a bit messed up."

"Are you okay?" she asked.

"Yeah, I'm okay," I said. "And best of all, I think I've removed the spirit from the house. You should be all right inside there now. I think it's gone."

She asked how I had done that. I just shrugged and said that I had made contact with it and encouraged it to leave. And that I'd gotten lucky.

"Was it a ghost then? A little girl who died here or something?"

"Hard to say exactly," I told her. "But it's gone now."

And with that I just gave her a hug and then walked to my car. It had been a long night, and I was bone-tired.

9
Returning the Spirit Back to the Trailer

I almost turned around—not because I wanted to go back into that metal box to see whether things were different, but because I'd forgotten my bag and empty water bottle. The water bottle was somewhere on the floor of the front room, so I figured that Tracy would come across it when she cleaned up the mess. She would either toss it or save it for me. Either way, it wasn't enough to warrant my return anytime soon.

The gym bag was also somewhere in that front room. If Tracy tossed out the bag, I could always get another. I really had no desire to go back there.

Besides, I might never need the gym bag and its contents again. Although I'd apparently succeeded in my third attempt at de-ghosting a house, I figured I was finished. I was ready to retire from Helen's noble line of work, as much as the world might need her sort of help. I decided that I wasn't ideally suited—either emotionally or otherwise— to be a ghost hunter. There were too many variables that I wasn't prepared to address.

Even going back wouldn't tell me much now, I reasoned. That

damned spirit could cloak itself and shape-shift, and, as a result, I probably hadn't been able to sense its presence much of the time. And I really was no match for it. I'd gotten lucky, tricking it into the mirror and luring it outside where, hopefully, it would stay.

The real question was whether it would leave the grounds entirely or simply linger near the front steps where I'd broken the mirror. I thought it unlikely that the spirit had literally gone into the mirror. Probably it had followed it with fascination, for it seemed to desire a physical presence, given the fact that, from time to time, it had assumed the physical form of a girl with blond curls. The creature itself though, whatever it was, clearly was not of our physical world.

Perhaps it was a malevolent ghost. I'd heard that some ghosts could be dangerous and cause physical harm. Helen's experience as a seasoned ghost hunter hadn't suggested that, however. Maybe she'd been lucky, but more likely she was simply very good at ghost hunting; much better than I'd ever be.

I got into my two-seat Triumph and decided to just let it go. I'd staked the property and salted the grounds. The spirit had been cast out. How could it re-enter the house? Why worry now? I'd done enough. That spirit was not getting back inside.

I turned the key to start the car, and the roadster roared to life with its throaty little growl. It was good to be back in my car, safely tucked away, the trials of the day over and done with. I couldn't wait to get home and draw a nice soothing bath in the quiet privacy of my own home.

The tires spun on loose gravel as I backed up to turn around and head back down the road. Even with the headlights on, it was hard to see, because the canopy of deep woods along that stretch of the road blocked out any starlight or moonlight. Also, the headlights of the sports car were set low to the ground. So what if I could hardly see the road I was driving on? I wasn't going to let any small concerns bother me. I was through being scared.

Still, I felt uneasy and a bit jumpy, and I couldn't relax in the car seat. Coupled with this, my head was spinning and beginning to throb. Why was I finding it so difficult to relax? My taxing ordeal was over.

I reached for the radio dial and turned on the radio. Flipping through the stations, I was met with static on each one. Nothing came in clearly up here on the mountain. I flicked off the radio and sighed. How long before I'd be home? I couldn't see my watch in the dark. It was getting late though.

Strangely, there were no mosquitoes or bugs of any sort splattering the windshield, as was usually the case on a warm summer night such as this one. I heard no sounds from the dense forest, which frequently came to life at night with nocturnal creatures.

I settled back more deeply into the seat and tried resting my head more squarely against the headrest, which felt awkward. I sensed a sudden chill in the air, and the car's heater didn't work very well. I wondered where in that little car I might have tossed my windbreaker. A jacket would help take the chill out of me. I started fumbling around. When I reached down to the floorboard beneath the passenger seat I lost control of the wheel and almost swerved off the mountain road.

Pulling the car over to the side, I stopped with the engine still running, put on the emergency brake, and began searching in earnest for my jacket. It wasn't in the car. Maybe it was in the car's back compartment? I got out and popped open the rear hatch of the Triumph to lift up the window, then pawed through a few things stashed in the back. There I found my jacket.

When I slammed the back hatch closed, however, the headlights went out! Now how could that have happened? I couldn't rationalize any correlation between the two events.

Then the headlights began flickering on and off. How frustrating, I thought. Darned English sports cars! They were infamous for their errant electrical systems. At one point I'd had the car completely rewired only to find that, when I got it back home, the wipers didn't work. It seemed that the electrical systems on these cars were not properly grounded (or something). A national sports car club in America had once offered all of its Lucas motorcar enthusiasts a special black Lucas T-shirt. White glow-in-the-dark lettering on the shirt read "Hail, Lucas—Prince of Darkness," a tacit wink to the many electrical problems that a Lucas motorcar was bound to have. As with other owners of this type of sports car, I found the electrical quirks in my Triumph to be one dark mystery.

I got back into the driver's seat and turned the lights off and then on again. Instead of functioning lights, however, the *wipers* started to go back and forth! I turned the light switch off again and sat, wondering how I was going to get home in the dark.

It occurred to me that I might simply have a bad battery connection or some minor problem—something under the hood (which, on this English car was called a "bonnet"), which I could actually fix. I decided to check the battery. When I propped up the hood, I groped in the darkness to find the battery cables. Hooking them up, I checked the connections, which seemed secure and the posts seemed tight. Well, of course! The car would start and *run* just fine. My problem was still unsolved, and I stood there stupidly with the bonnet up, studying the engine, wondering what to do.

Suddenly the horn started blowing. I have no idea why. It just started blaring in my face and it wouldn't stop. I reached over it to one side of the engine and traced my hands back to the connecting wire then pulled on it until it gave way. Silence. No more horn. Good, I thought, I fixed it.

But where did that leave me?

Just then, a car came around the corner at high speed, the driver blaring his horn as he swerved to miss me. Gravel spun onto my car and me. The car shot past and disappeared around the next turn on the mountain road.

This was getting dangerous, I decided. And I was getting worried.

Strange how, just minutes ago, I'd been frightened by the spirit and relieved to be going down the road. Now I longed to be off the road and back up the mountain!

Because Tracy's trailer was closer than my house at this point, I decided to turn the car around and head back up the hill. I figured I could drive on the rough road in the dark if I drove slowly and cautiously. It seemed the safest thing to do.

When I turned the car around to head back up the hill, however, the lights came back on.

"Huh?" I said to myself. That was weird.

So while the lights were still working, I turned the car around again and headed back down the mountain. I sputtered along the gravel road at a good clip, and figured I was in the clear, given that I was warm and the car seemed fully functional again. Surely my luck would hold out for another fifteen or twenty minutes until I reached my Brightwood home.

At that moment my back began to feel odd. I twitched my shoulders a little, figuring that I must have developed a muscle cramp somewhere along the way. After I did that, I felt a sort of tingle all the way from the back of my head down my spine. Odd, I thought. What's this about?

Then I felt something touching my shoulders. Instinctively I looked up, but nothing had fallen on me. I wasn't riding in an open convertible. I reached up with one hand to brush my shoulder. I used the other hand to brush the other shoulder. There was nothing there.

And now I felt nothing on my shoulders. How strange! My mind was working overtime as I zipped down the gravel road.

Just then I felt something on my neck. Something was choking me!

I tried to stay focused while I fought for oxygen to breathe, and, at the same time, I slammed on the brakes, causing gravel to spit everywhere. The tires fought for traction on the loose surface of the road, and the car fishtailed madly as it skidded to a halt. With the lights on and the motor running, I reached up behind me with both hands to grasp whatever was choking me.

As I did this, the choking stopped.

I was almost afraid to look around. I turned on the overhead dome light but saw nothing in the front seat and nothing on the floor of the car. I looked on the dash and inside the glove box and still found nothing. I turned around to look behind the seat. Lots of things were stashed behind the two bucket seats, but nothing looked suspect or out of place.

With a sickening feeling I checked out the windows and then examined the roof of the car. Nada.

Then I realized that the evil spirit in the house had followed me into the car! It was punishing me for what I had done to it back at the trailer.

What could I do now? I was fresh out of tricks. I had followed my training to the letter, step by step. This spirit, if a ghost, should by rights now be banished. Instead, it was camped in my car, tormenting me. There was apparently no way to get rid of this malevolent being, whatever it was. Indeed, it might follow and hound me until my dying day.

But then I began to reason with myself. One always has choices, I told myself. No matter how dark and narrow the road gets, a person always has choices, undesirable as they might seem. But what were *my* choices? I could think only of two. I could take this brooding spirit down the road with me and let it follow me into my house and my life. Or—I could return it to where I had originally found it.

I'm not proud of the decision I made that night. I pointed the car back toward Tracy's trailer and returned to her place in the woods.

There was no further incident on the ride there. I felt no other hands upon me, and the car operated without any problems. It almost seemed as though the malevolent spirit had left me and departed from the car—but I knew otherwise. My guess was it was happy that I was returning it back to its haunt, and I imagined it was rather enjoying its triumphant ride home.

The sports car sputtered its way up the gravel drive to the trailer and came to a resting place some feet away. Everyone had gone inside except for the dog, which sat at the bottom of the front steps.

Tracy had swept the glass off the steps, and it almost appeared as though the shattering of the mirror and the botched exorcism had never occurred.

Slowly I walked up the steps, and stood at the top of them for a moment before knocking softly on the door.

"It's me," I said. "I'm back. Didn't get too far."

Tracy opened the door and gave me a look of surprise.

"What's wrong?" she asked me.

I just looked at her, not knowing how to say what I had to say.

"I didn't get too far," I repeated. "Things started going wrong with the car. First I didn't think anything of it. The lights went out, then came on again. The windshield wipers came on for no reason. Then the horn started to blow. But it wasn't just the car . . ." I said, looking at her with a deadpan expression.

"Oh, no!" she said.

"Oh, yes! It came home with me. It got in the car and left here with me. And that's not the worst part . . ."

Todd and Missy, who had been standing a few feet inside the trailer now moved closer to the door to hear my every word.

"It started to strangle me in the car," I told them, "while I was driving. I had to stop."

"What are you going to do?" Tracy asked.

"I don't know what else to do," I said. "I can't drive like that, with it trying to strangle me. I probably wouldn't even make it home."

I looked past the door to the front room of the trailer. Everything that had been scattered on the floor had been collected and put away. The place looked neat and peaceful again.

"Look, I'm sorry," I said. "I have no other choice. I don't know what else to do. I have to put it back in here."

"No!" Todd said. "You can't do that!"

Todd's thinning black hair was a mess. He was a scruffy, gaunt man with a lot of bad luck, living in a borrowed trailer, and driving a wreck of a car. I guessed that he had been through a lot in his life. How could I put him through another ordeal?

"I have no other option," I said quietly. "It rode with me in the car. But when I drove back here, I didn't feel it anymore. The car didn't act crazy. Look, maybe it didn't even come back here with me," I told them, beginning to backslide a bit.

"How can we be sure?" Tracy asked.

"I don't know. I tried to remove it from your home. I don't exactly know where it is right now."

"She wants to play with me!" Missy said. "She misses me."

Tracy grabbed her daughter's hand and gave her a shake. "It's a dangerous thing!" she told her. "You don't want her around anymore!"

"Maybe you're in the clear now," I said somewhat cautiously. "Again, I don't know. Maybe I brought it back here. I hope not. But you need to be on your guard. It seemed pretty angry."

"We got no place else to go," Todd said.

"We could sleep in the car," Tracy suggested.

"No more sleeping in the car," Todd said. "Besides, we're supposed to be caretakers here. That's the deal."

Actually, the deal as I understood it, called for Todd—with his background as a night watchman—to house-sit and maintain the mobile home. In exchange, he and his family were allowed to live there rent-free. It was unlikely that they'd be able to afford another place to live, since Todd no longer had his night watchman job and now collected groceries at the local food shelf. If they wanted a roof over their heads, they were stuck here. In addition, the owner of this forlorn property in the middle of the woods had probably waited a long time to find someone willing to maintain the house for him. After all, it *was* haunted.

"Well, come on in," Tracy said. "I'll heat up some water for herb tea."

I had hoped never to enter that trailer again, but I gingerly crossed the threshold and reentered the structure. "Where were you guys living before you moved here?" I asked them.

"Oh, we had a small apartment in town," Tracy replied. "It was pretty tiny. We wanted to move."

"Maybe you should think about going back there if you can," I told her.

"No, we couldn't move back there," she said. "Not now."

"No vacancies?" I asked.

"We ain't got the money," Todd intoned rather flatly. "Rent here is free."

"Well, where else have you lived?" I asked. "Anyplace else you might consider?"

Tracy handed me a cup of hot tea.

"We've lived all around," she said. "Sometimes in the woods, camping out. Can't do that now, with the cold weather coming. Maybe if it was springtime."

"Do you have any relatives you can stay with? Friends perhaps?" I asked.

"Car's the problem," Todd said. "Everybody we know—anywhere that might take us in, even for a short while, would be a far piece from here. Don't think that old car would make it. They're too many things wrong with it."

I didn't know all that was wrong with their old Plymouth, but I had seen them stranded on the highway pass at one point. Another time I'd stopped to help Todd with a flat tire, which was completely bald. The only spare he had was a "doughnut" tire that he used to get himself to a repair station.

"We'll be okay. It's probably out there somewhere," Tracy said, pointing out the front door. "You did remove it from the house, and that's good, right?"

I looked at her and sighed. How did I know? "You can see how it goes tonight," I suggested. "Who knows? It might be okay. You'll know soon enough, right?"

Todd looked peeved. "But I thought you got rid of it," he exclaimed. "How can it be back here?"

"Oh, Todd!" said Tracy. "He did his best. Let's not get excited before we know there's a problem."

I offered to walk through the trailer and check things out—to see if I could sense the dark spirit anywhere.

"Will that work?" Tracy said.

I explained that I had had trouble tuning in to it initially but then had finally been able to perceive it.

Missy was looking under her bedcovers for her sketchbook and seemed pretty excited to show us something. "I want to show you how she looks!" she exclaimed, still searching for her pad. "I know her very well, and she's a sweet little girl. And pretty, too. She likes me and plays with me all the time!"

Unable to locate her ever-present sketchbook, Missy now sprawled out on the floor, trying to reach under her bed to find the book.

"She doesn't really look that way," I told her. "I've seen the way she really looks. And it's not pretty."

Tracy grabbed my arm and pulled me away from the girl to talk privately. "What *does* it actually look like?" she asked me.

I made a face and hesitated to answer. "You don't really want to know," I said.

But she insisted on hearing it all. Todd soon joined us.

"It isn't human," I said simply.

"Of course not!" Todd said. "It's some kind of ghost."

"That's what I thought," I answered. "But it's like no kind of ghost I've ever seen or heard about."

"What do you mean?" Tracy asked.

I swallowed hard. She punched my arm a couple of times to prompt a response. We closed ranks in a circle so Missy wouldn't hear us.

"Not human," I repeated for Todd and Tracy. "A ghost is supposed to be a person or an animal that's died, right? It should resemble that person. This thing doesn't look anything like a person."

"A little girl with golden curls is the way Missy always describes her," Tracy interjected.

"Maybe she appears that way to Missy," I said. "I saw something entirely different."

"Well, maybe you didn't see the ghost that Missy's always talking about," Tracy said.

How could I tell these sweet, back-to-nature people that something hideous had been haunting their home while they were asleep at night? I didn't want to tell them everything I'd seen, but now knew I had to.

"Okay, I saw a blond girl with curls, about eight or nine years old," I told them.

"See!" Tracy said.

"No, that wasn't all," I said. "There's more to it. I saw a hideous creature, a dark and brooding creature with red eyes. Old and grisly. And then it shape-shifted into the blond girl with curls."

Missy interrupted our circle with a whine. "I can't find my book!" she said. "I wanted to show you how my special friend looks. She's so pretty."

I spun around to face her. "Listen," I cautioned, "that thing is no pretty little girl! You need to stay away from it! If it comes back, you should ignore it, okay? Pretend you don't see it!"

"Why?" she argued. "You don't know her. Not like I do."

"I think that thing has been tricking you, Missy," I said. "It appears the way you want to see her. It's probably not even a girl. It disguises itself."

"No!" she continued. "She's not wearing any disguise! I would know if she was wearing a mask or something. She's not!"

"It's not exactly like that," I tried to explain. "It can change the way it looks—turn into something it's not."

"You mean like magic?" Missy said.

"Yes, black magic," I said.

"Cool!" she answered.

"Missy!" Tracy curtailed. "That's not cool! That's evil. And it's dangerous to be around that creature."

"Creature?" Missy asked.

I was stumped here. I didn't know exactly how to describe it.

"Just stay clear of her, if you can," Tracy instructed. "We don't know what it is, but it isn't safe for you to play with it anymore, okay?"

Missy flopped down on her bed face-down, in a pout.

"You gonna check the house for us?" Todd asked. "I'd do it myself, but I don't know exactly what I'm looking for . . ."

"All right," I agreed. "I'll give it the once-over and go room to room to see if I can sense anything."

"At least there aren't many rooms to check," Tracy offered. "Just this room and our bedroom at the end."

"And the hallway," I added. "Don't forget the hallway leading back to your bedroom. That's where I saw it before."

"Really?" Tracy said. "Just standing there in that dark hallway?"

"It was sitting on the dryer," I said. "Or was it the washer? Anyway, it was just sitting there, glaring at me."

"Creepy," Todd said.

"Yeah, it creeped me out, that's for sure!" I said. "Actually, I think it was waiting there for me. Like a trap. I opened the gate and walked down the narrow hallway. Then when I looked up, there it was—like it was lying in wait."

I asked all three of them to step outside on the porch for a couple of minutes so that I could work alone and try to tune in to the spirit again, if it was present. I needed the area cleared so I could fully concentrate on what I was doing. I told them not to come back inside until I came out to get them.

Once the door was shut and I was alone in the trailer, I began to sweat. Honestly, I wasn't sure that I could go through it all again.

I heard a knocking on the door. It opened and in stepped Tracy.

"Sorry," she said. "I just wondered if you wanted your bag. Your bag of tricks—isn't that what you call it?"

She started to walk toward the kitchen counter where I saw the gym bag resting. Right, I thought to myself. This bag won't help me now. I'm fresh out of tricks.

"No, I'm fine," I said. "Won't need that." I motioned with a wave of one hand for her to scoot back outside.

I sat on Missy's bed again with my feet firmly grounded on the floor and my posture erect, trying to clear my mind to listen. Because of all that I'd seen and been through already, this was a difficult thing to do. But finally I reached a still, quiet place deep inside me, even though my stomach was churning. Now it was time to empty all thoughts and sensations and try to focus only on making contact with the strange being.

The room grew so quiet that I was completely lost inside of myself for a moment. I saw a blank screen in my mind's eye and began to fill it with the image of the creature I'd seen. I visualized the little girl with curls and listened with a greater awareness.

Nothing.

I stood up and walked to the hallway, unhooking the childproof gate. I walked past the gate and into the corridor. Darn, I'd forgotten a flashlight, and the corridor was as dark as could be.

I stumbled for a moment, then stopped to try to adjust my eyes to the limited light from the room behind me. I began to advance, feeling my way along the wall. When I got to the washer and dryer I slipped by them. Fortunately there was nothing perched atop the washer or the dryer this time—not that I could see, anyway.

I entered the back bedroom and flipped on the overhead light. Looking around, everything looked the same as it had earlier in the evening. I sat on Tracy and Todd's big bed and again went deep within, trying to tune in to the creature's vibrations. But again there was nothing. I felt no tingling sensation or weird vibes, and I decided to leave. Leave now while you can get out safely, I told myself.

I exited the trailer to find Tracy, Todd, Missy, and their dog huddled at the bottom of the steps, waiting to reenter the house.

"Is it okay to go in there now?" Tracy asked feebly.

"I didn't see, hear, or sense anything this time," I said. "I think the house is clean."

"How can you be sure?" Todd asked.

"I can't," I said. "But it seems okay now. Maybe that thing left you. Maybe it's out here somewhere. I don't know. But it doesn't feel like it's inside your house now."

The three of them trudged back up the stairs. It had been a long night.

Tracy thanked me and invited me over to hunt mushrooms with them in the coming days, given that the orange beauties were presently quite abundant in nearby Rhododendron. I waved as I left.

As I took my leave I noticed that the dog remained outside. "Is the dog not allowed inside?" I asked. It struck me that nobody ever addressed it by name or played with it.

"Oh, he's just a watchdog," Todd said. "He stays outside to guard the place."

That's a good idea, I thought. You need a watchdog here.

Walking back to my car, I began to feel the presence of the spirit again. It was out here somewhere.

10
Consequences of the Trailer Haunting

Naturally, I felt apprehensive about driving back down the hill with the dark spirit still at large. It had been hiding in my car, and I had seemed to sense it on the grounds outside of the trailer again. Maybe it had never left the car, because it hadn't seemed to be present in the trailer. And even if it had gotten out of my roadster at Tracy's place, it could have jumped back into my car to torment me again. That seemed highly probable based on what had happened to me earlier. Clearly I had made it angry. But I also reasoned that the trailer was its chosen haunt, and no doubt it would prefer to remain there.

Anyway, I had to venture home, as it was getting late and the option of staying at Tracy's trailer certainly held no appeal for me.

For the first mile or two of the ride back to Brightwood, I worried about what actions I might take if the dark spirit tried to strangle me in the car again. If that were the case it might take a supreme effort to slow down the car and pull it safely to a stop alongside the road. How would I be able to accomplish that if I was being strangled, given that my natural instinct for survival would be to reach around my neck to remove the creature's deadly grip?

But was its grip around a person's throat really deadly? Todd had told me it had attempted to strangle him in his sleep, but he had clearly survived the attacks. So maybe this malevolent spirit wasn't a killer. Maybe it just wanted to scare people off—older people, primarily.

Then I remembered the names and dates carved into the tree beside the trailer, which no doubt were dogs' names and the dates of their demise. I doubted whether all of them had died of old age. And it was unlikely that cars had run them down out there in the middle of nowhere on that private driveway. No, there was something evil and perhaps deadly about this dark spirit, whatever it was.

About halfway home I calmed down and decided that the spirit probably hadn't returned with me in the car. I felt I was finally in the clear, for I sensed nothing odd around me, and nothing unusual had happened on my ride home this time. Soon I would be safe and sound in my own bed, far from the trailer and all it possessed.

As I sputtered into the carport in front of my double A-frame home, I just sat for a minute after turning off the key. Everything was so tranquil. I could hear the late-summer crickets and night creatures climbing through the branches of the Douglas fir trees tucked tightly around my cottage. There was a little light from the heavens above shining down on the street, and my house looked very calm, as though it was peacefully sleeping. Soon I would be sleeping peacefully too, I thought. Would I dream of the spirit after my eyes were closed?

I made a vow to myself then and there, sitting alone in my car under the moon, that I was finished with ghost hunting. I had tried three times and had struck out all three. I wouldn't need the gym bag with its penny nails, kosher salt, and vial of holy water. I most certainly had no need to carry mirrors around. I was retired, for I had failed to de-ghost houses.

Or had I? For all I knew, I *might* have banished the ghost from the old brick church in Portland. I apparently had been successful in turning back the spirits that haunted my house and hovered above its skylights. And the spirit in Tracy's trailer had been removed from the trailer. Those were measures of success that might allow me to sleep soundly at night. Lord knows, I was tired enough to sleep forever *that* night!

Opening the car door and hoisting myself out of the low bucket seat, I headed for the side door next to the carport. I had forgotten to leave on the porch light, but that was okay. I could see clearly, and I walked up the steps with my keys in one hand.

Wait a minute, I suddenly thought. What if the spirit had been riding back with me and I had been unable to detect its presence? It had gotten into my car before and was out to get me for tricking it back at the trailer house.

No, I was safe now, I reasoned with myself. Stop making things up.

Still, it was hard to open the door to the house, given the possibility that the spirit might enter it with me.

When I woke up the next morning everything seemed fine. I decided to stop worrying that the spirit was pursuing me. It was done with me—or so I hoped.

I more or less just went through the motions at work for the next day or two, worrying about nothing more mysterious or frightening than house fires or highway accidents. As always in the newspaper business, deadlines loomed. Presses started and stopped on tight schedules, so I did my part to keep things on track at the paper, returning home only to eat and sleep.

After a couple of days I thought about visiting Tracy and her family to see how things were going for them after the spirit extraction. Admittedly, I had been hesitant about dropping in because I really just wanted to put the entire matter out of my mind. The responsible course of action, however, would be to check back with them to see what was happening, if anything. Besides, Tracy had mentioned mushroom hunting, and I was always ready for that.

So when Saturday morning rolled around, I gave myself the day off and zipped back up the old fire trail to their mobile home in the forest.

Tracy stood outside drying herbs while Missy played nearby, drawing in her sketch pad. It was comforting that she had found it again after that crazy night of paranormal activity inside their metal home. The dog was walking around, sniffing the dying embers of a campfire out front. I didn't see the car, so I assumed that Todd had left.

Hearing me pull my car to a gravel-spitting stop and slam the door shut, Tracy looked up from her herbal preparations and frowned.

Oh, dear, what's wrong now? I wondered. I slowed my walk, taking as much time to reach her as possible.

"Hi," she said. "We had a rough night here last night."

I looked at her daughter for clues, but she ignored us and continued to draw.

"In what sense?" I asked Tracy.

"The same thing," she replied. "It's back."

I glanced quickly up at the trailer house. It looked peaceful enough—from the outside.

"Okay, tell me," I said.

She just looked at me in a puzzled sort of way. "I thought you got rid of it the other night," she said. "You got it out of the house, right?"

"I tried," I said, a little defensively. "I'm sure it left the house. But I couldn't completely get rid of it. When I left, I think it was outside your house. It's possible that it moved back inside."

"Oh, it did!" Tracy said.

"So tell me what happened," I said.

Tracy just looked at me with a sick sort of expression. "It tried to strangle Todd again!" she told me. "Really freaked him out. He jumped out of bed, threw on his pants, and drove out of here! Hasn't been home since."

"Did it try to put hands on you too?" I asked.

"Me? No, I got out of bed and sat up all night, most of it outside on the porch."

I looked at Missy, still drawing quietly, absorbed in her own little world.

"Missy, did you see the blond girl with the curls?" I asked her.

Preoccupied, she took a moment to ponder the question. "Oh, I've seen her lots of times!" she said. "I saw her just last night!"

"What did she do? Did she do anything or say anything to you?"

Missy smiled. "She's sweet," Missy said. "She found my book and gave it back to me." She held up her sketch pad. "Want to see what she drew in the book?" Missy asked. "She drew a picture for me."

My eyes bulged. A spirit that drew pictures? I moved closer to Missy.

She opened her sketchbook to a page toward the back and held the book up for me to see.

She held it wide open, so that I could see both the right and left pages. There was a purpose to her showing me both pages at once—the drawing she was showing me covered both panels.

"See the picture she drew for me?!" Missy said.

The drawing was crude and stark, done in bold black strokes. Where the lines were drawn, other lines had been added to trace over the initial lines for emphasis. The picture looked like three people—or rather, stick figures of three people. There were two tall people on the left side, the shorter of which had long hair. I assumed that these figures were meant to represent two adults. A shorter stick figure, also with long hair, filled the right panel. I understood that to represent Missy. These were images of the family, separated by the gutter between the pages. On the corner of the left panel where the parents were drawn was a small dog, lying down. This, no doubt, was the family dog.

There was a sort of halo or arch over the girl in the right panel, resembling a form of protection over her head. There was nothing similar over the images of the two adults in the left panel. Instead, crude slash marks had been drawn across their images as though to cross them out of the picture.

In all, I found the rough depictions to be both revealing and alarming.

"What do you think the picture shows?" I asked Missy.

The smile disappeared from her face. "I think she drew my parents, me, and the dog," she replied. "That's what it looks like to me."

"Well, you're probably the best judge of that," I said, "since she drew it for you."

Missy frowned. "I think she wants to get rid of Mom and Todd. She crossed them out. She has them far away from me and crossed out. And she put a cover over me."

"What about the dog in the picture?" I asked. "Is he sleeping, or dead?"

She looked up slowly with sad eyes. "I dunno," she said. "Maybe."

Tracy snatched the book from her. "That's a horrible picture—not fit for young eyes!" she told her daughter. "I'm putting this book away. It's already caused too much trouble!"

Missy pleaded, but to no avail. Tracy walked into the trailer with the book in hand. She returned promptly. Missy asked where she'd put it, but Tracy ignored her.

"So how do we get this thing out of my house now?" Tracy asked me.

I shook my head. "I gave it my best shot," I said. "I used all the tools—all the tricks I had. I used everything I was taught by a pretty experienced and successful ghost exterminator."

"So you do think it's a ghost?" Tracy asked, giving Missy a glance to see if she'd upset her.

"I don't know," I answered plainly. "I wish I did. One thing I do know is that it's not behaving like a normal ghost. Or else it's a pretty powerful dark spirit that's just too much to handle. Either way, I don't know what else I can do."

"But how did it get back in the house?" Tracy persisted.

"Right," I said. "I did salt the property and stake the four corners to keep it out. Once it was out of the house, it shouldn't have been able to get back in."

"If it's just a ghost . . ." she said.

"If it's a just a ghost," I agreed. "But maybe it's like a super ghost—a really powerful dark spirit of a departed soul that once lived here and now just won't leave."

"Somebody who died here?" she asked me.

"Maybe," I said. "I don't really know. I don't know what it is or how to get rid of it."

"Wonderful," she said sarcastically.

"I think you should seriously think about moving out," I told Tracy. "Not just out of the trailer, but away from these grounds. Get out while you can. It could get worse."

"Really?" she said. "How could it get any worse?"

"Let's not even go there," I told her. "I don't want to think about that."

Tracy looked even more upset, and I decided to level with her. "It could get violent, or else make your lives really difficult. You don't need that. It's just not worth it."

Tracy squatted on her haunches, native-style. Then she sighed. "We have nowhere else to go. And there are three of us, plus the dog. Who'd take us in?"

I shook my head; how did I know? "Must be somebody. Give it some thought."

"If it weren't getting into the colder months, we might camp in the woods. We've done it before, but only in the summer, which now is almost over. We'll see frost soon. And we live pretty high up on a mountain where it gets really cold."

I thought about Mount Hood's permanent snowcap and an early winter when I'd been snowed in with busted, frozen pipes for eight days.

"Yeah," I said finally.

Our attention was diverted to the road at the edge of the property where Todd was pulling up in the car. Tracy and I stopped talking about things we didn't really want to discuss to watch Todd get out of the car and approach us. He had an angry look on his face.

"I suppose she told you what happened last night!" Todd said to me. I nodded.

"So you know. Thank you very much, smart newspaper man! All you did was make it mad! And *you* don't have to live with it. You can just get in your little sports car and drive home, snug as a bug. Well, we ain't that lucky! We're stuck here!"

"I'm sorry, Todd," I told him. "I did try. I really did. I used every trick I had and everything I've been taught. They should have worked."

Tracy held out an arm, as though to hold Todd back. "He thinks we should move out—go somewhere else," Tracy told her husband.

"Oh? Like where?" Todd said. "We got no place to go. Think about it, woman!"

"The little blond girl loves me!" Missy interjected.

"Shut up, you!" Todd snarled at her. "You put us right in the middle of this, your mother and me."

"Oh, Todd!" Tracy chided. "It's not her fault."

I felt a bit awkward being in the center of this family squabble.

"Well, I probably should be going," I said. "I was thinking we might go 'shrooming,' but it looks like you have a lot to think about today."

"Maybe tomorrow, Sunday, afternoon," Tracy said quietly.

"Right," I agreed. "Well, think about maybe finding another place, if you can. Family? Friends? Maybe call a church or two in town for ideas. Just to play it safe, right?"

Nobody responded, so I walked quietly to my car. Nobody said good-bye as I left.

I spent the weekend at the office trying to get caught up. I worked there all day Saturday, went out for a quick bite to eat, and then returned to the office. Turning on the TV, I watched the late weekend wrap-up news show from Portland, lingering at the same time over some odds and ends at my desk. It was getting late. I was ready to wind my way home to catch a few hours of sleep before returning to work the next morning.

In the newspaper office, even on the weekend with most of the staff gone, the police and fire scanner was typically on. The rule was never to turn it off, because someone might forget to turn it on again when we returned to work. If this were to happen we might miss some newsworthy emergency. When there *was* an emergency, we would hastily grab our camera gear and dash to our cars to chase whatever emergency assistance vehicles were screaming down the road. Sometimes it would prove to be nothing—a false alarm or something insignificant. Other times, however, we would encounter a real catastrophe and need to be at the scene immediately.

The scanner went wild late that night with a major emergency, catching me totally off guard. It broadcast a fire alarm, dispatching trucks to some fire that was raging up the mountain. Details were sketchy, but it had been spotted by a neighbor who lived some distance away. Given that the fire was in the middle of the national forest, it was of major concern. All the town's fire trucks were dispatched, as well as a police car. The dispatcher was calling out directions based on sketchy details.

Heck, I thought. I can follow them with directions like that. In fact, I could even tag behind at a safe distance with my camera and big strobe light. I grabbed a camera bag and a charged-up strobe on my way out the door.

It was easy to follow the emergency response vehicles. They formed a screaming caravan heading out of town on the main street and ascending up the mountain pass. I got safely behind the last one in line and followed as closely as I dared. Halfway up the mountain, all of the response vehicles stopped to assess where they were in relation to the fire. They seemed lost and uncertain about how to continue. I had no scanner in my sports car but figured the emergency vehicles were getting updated directions from the dispatcher. Apparently they didn't have a proper address. This was a rural area and one that was hard to negotiate, given the dense forest that engulfed the entire mountain. With the fire in the middle of the national forest, I assumed that trucks from the other side of the mountain would be reinforcing these local responders soon.

The responders started winding up the mountain, making me realize that we were headed up toward Tracy's house. I hoped that the fire wouldn't spread to her place, where the trees were very thick. A late-summer forest fire could move very quickly.

Our winding ascent finally brought us to a clearing where the road became straight. We were headed in the general direction of Tracy's trailer. I only wished that I could notify Tracy and Todd to get in their car and clear out now, before the fire got near them. But they had no phone.

The fire trucks ahead of me were throwing up quite a cloud of dust on that mountain road, and it was all I could do to keep up with them in my little car. When we came to the gravel road off the main road the trucks stopped there. At this, I really started to worry. This was the drive to Tracy's place. As the trucks started pulling onto the gravel road, I hoped that they'd taken a wrong turn. Tracy had enough problems; she didn't need a forest fire to contend with as well.

At the end of the drive I saw Tracy and Missy standing in front of a very burned-out trailer. It had been totally destroyed. The fire had run its course through the metal box and was almost through burning. A few flames came out of the windows here and there. It was a total mess.

I rushed to Tracy and her daughter.

"My god, what happened here?" I asked them.

Tracy fell on my shoulders and started to sob. Missy drew near and pressed against the two of us for comfort.

"I don't know how it caught fire," Tracy said between sobs. "Suddenly the whole place was ablaze. We barely got out alive."

"Where's Todd?" I asked.

"He got out. Went crazy. Said he couldn't take it here anymore. Got in the car and drove off."

"Won't the firemen want to talk with him?" I asked.

"Why?" she said. "He doesn't know anything. None of us do! The trailer just erupted in fire all of a sudden, and there was fire everywhere. It was crazy. Just crazy."

"Did you get any of your things out?" I asked.

"No," Tracy said. "No time. No time for anything. It was so sudden."

I looked around at the destruction. No trees had burned, just the trailer. Tracy's herbs were still out to dry. Something was missing, though.

"Where's your dog?" I asked. "Did it run away?"

Missy started to cry.

"It was burned in the fire," Tracy said. "Crazy thing was the way it got trapped. It was trapped under the trailer. Tied with a chain! We never tied that dog up. Never."

Quickly out of nowhere the image of that old tree with all the dogs' names carved into it flashed into my head. One more name and date to add to the list, I thought. That is, if the poor dog even had a name.

The fire captain approached us and took off his helmet. "The fire's going to be under control shortly, ma'am," he told Tracy. "There was nobody left inside, was there?"

Our eyes turned to the firefighters who were sorting through the debris. "No," she replied. "Only our dog. He was tied up under the house. But we never tied him up. I don't know how he got tied up. Chained up, actually."

"We need to know how the fire started, ma'am," the captain asked.

"No idea," said Tracy.

"Did you have anything on the stove or in the oven, maybe?" he probed.

"No. We didn't cook anything for dinner. We cooked outside on the campfire."

"Maybe you had a candle burning somewhere and forgot about it?"

"No."

"Your propane tank—did you notice any leaking, or have you recently filled it?"

Tracy shook her head firmly.

"Well, ma'am," said the captain, "we'll probably need to do some sort of investigation. Who owns the trailer?"

Tracy wrote down the owner's name on the captain's clipboard, along with a contact phone number.

"How can I get in touch with you? I'll have more questions after you've had a chance to sort things out here."

"You can reach me through him," Tracy said, pointing to me. "I have no phone. I have no house."

After I gave the captain my card, I loaded Tracy and Missy into my car. It was too small for all three of us to ride up front, so Missy had to crunch her body into the back hatch area, which was really nothing more than a narrow flat storage area. She and her mother had very little to take with them other than a bag of herbs Tracy had outside the trailer.

I asked them to stay with me until they sorted things out. There was no going back to the trailer, which was demolished and probably wouldn't be replaced, even with a successful insurance claim by the absentee owner.

Todd failed to show at my house to collect Tracy or his stepdaughter or even to see them. Probably he was just driving around in that wreck of a car, if it hadn't broken down again.

✝

The next day a fire marshal dropped by the house. He wasn't one of the personnel who had responded to the fire at the trailer but a state investigator dressed in a starched white uniform.

He quizzed Tracy for some time in my living room. I sat in on some of the investigation, but he asked no questions of me other than to inquire about my connection with the family and to question me as to how I had happened to appear at the fire that night. When I explained that I was a local newspaperman who just followed the trucks with a camera and knew the family, he seemed satisfied with that.

He asked Tracy a number of questions about Todd. He wanted to know why he'd fled the scene and why he was no longer with the family. I suppose it did look suspicious to an outsider, but I didn't believe Todd to be in any way responsible for the tragic fire.

Before the fire marshal left he asked Tracy to sign a statement he'd written based on her responses. He handed her the clipboard and pen. She started to read it, then just shook her head and signed. He nodded good-bye cordially before ducking out the door and getting into his white SUV.

The next day a social worker visited and asked Tracy a lot of questions about Missy. She also wanted to know about Todd and his relationship with his stepdaughter in particular. It was hard to see where this approach was headed, but at the end of the visit the woman told Tracy that Missy needed to be put into high school in town. She declared that Tracy wasn't supplying adequately supervised homeschooling that followed a defined, formal curriculum. Tracy's approach to homeschooling was basic herbal training, lessons in mushroom hunting, and how to work a good campfire. These were all good things to know, to be sure, but they left a lot of room for formal academic concerns such as reading, writing, and arithmetic.

The social worker also questioned whether Missy had been properly sheltered following the fire, given that the family had no home or permanent address of its own. She apparently failed to see my couch as a proper home environment. All of this government intervention was beginning to rattle Tracy, who preferred to live in the backwoods on her own terms.

Missy entered the conversation and stated that she would love to go to high school in town. Her mother's arguments against social pro-gramming and government interference didn't seem to faze her daugh-ter's enthusiasm for social interaction with the kids who lived in town.

"Well, how are we going to get you to school in town if we're way up the mountain here in the middle of nowhere?" Tracy countered.

"He could drive me to school in the morning when he goes to work in town," Missy said, pointing at me.

"But he doesn't come home when school is over," her mother noted. "He's busy *working* in the afternoon."

The social worker saw her opening here. "Perhaps we can place your daughter with a nice family in town so that she can attend school," she said. "You'd be with the family just temporarily," she told Missy, "until things are more stable."

"You mean like a foster home?" Tracy asked gloomily.

"Well, we'll see what we can arrange," the social worker replied. "There are a lot of nice families in town who might be able to give your daughter a good place to live while attending school. Let me see what I can do."

Missy jumped up with a shriek of excitement at the prospect of dances, activities, friends, and boys.

"Exactly how old are you?" she asked Missy.

"She's sixteen," Tracy said. "I don't have her birth certificate though."

"See!" the social worker said triumphantly "She probably has just a couple years of school left, depending on how well she tests and the grade she's placed in. High school years are the most important years of a young girl's life! You don't want her to miss out on that."

The very next morning the social worker returned to my house.

She gave Tracy a piece of paper that authorized the county to take custody of her daughter and then escorted the girl to her car as Tracy watched in horror. Missy seemed happy to be moving to town and going to high school, something she told me she'd wanted to do for quite some time now.

When Tracy heard nothing from or about her daughter the next day, despite sitting impatiently by my phone, she packed a small makeshift bag and headed out the door. She told me that she was going to take a little trip. She said she might visit Orcas Island and Louis, given that I'd told her how much visiting him had meant to me. I made sure Tracy had a few provisions, but she didn't want much. I wondered how far she'd get, hitchhiking to the San Juan Islands from where we were in western Washington state.

She was gone for two weeks, then showed up on my doorstep one night after I got home from work. It was getting cold outside now, and I urged her to stay with me for a while to avoid the brunt of the winter's harsh weather.

Tracy said she had made it all the way to Orcas Island, sleeping alongside the road between rides. Now that she had returned to Mount Hood, she wanted to get her daughter back. Apparently that wouldn't prove easy for her, given that she had no visible means of support and no home.

Todd called the house shortly after Tracy returned from Orcas Island. He was in the county jail. He and Tracy had a heated conversation, and he got her pretty riled up. Apparently Missy had made comments about her relationship with Todd to the social worker, and that was part of why she had been spirited away from her mother as well. Based on what Missy had said about Todd, the county was urging the girl to make formal charges against him, charges that he had abused her. County officials had apparently quizzed Missy about Todd's possible involvement with the mysterious fire too, but Todd said no charges against him were pending on that front.

Tracy tried to convince the county to release Todd and set the record straight, as she put it. Her phone calls didn't seem to convince them to release her husband. She cried and pleaded as she tried to reason with them.

Even though Tracy was apparently upset with Todd for the situation she now found herself in, she defended him vehemently against charges that he had abused Missy. "Todd even changed that girl's diapers when she was a baby," she argued. "Todd isn't her natural father, but he's been just like a father to her and would never do anything to hurt her!"

Missy ended up living with a very nice married couple and their son who lived near town. As luck would have it, I knew this family and had been to their home. They served as resident managers of a state park near the Columbia River gorge. They lived in the resident caretaker's cottage, which provided Missy with plenty of opportunity to gather herbs and sketch on the weekends when she was out of school. When I looked in on her, she seemed quite happy.

You just never know how things will end up. For Tracy, who was homeless and had lost her family, things didn't end well. She wandered around from place to place. I'm unaware exactly when the county released Todd, because I never saw or heard from him again. Missy seemed happy with her new family; she had many friends at school and was now in a stimulating environment. I did wonder whether anyone had ever buried their dog, who had burned to death in the fire. Perhaps Tracy had wandered back there one day to carve the poor dog's name and date of death into the tree.

I knew that I never wanted to visit that place again. It was most definitely haunted.

11
The Unseen Problems
with Ghosts
and Hauntings

Attempting to clear haunted houses and buildings can become dangerous, as I learned firsthand on the mountain. In some cases the effort might even prove futile. Beyond this physical world where we live our mundane lives, nonmaterial beings of the spirit world can assume many identities and harbor agendas that are beyond our scope to understand. Many of them are not deceased people who have difficulties moving on but spirits who were *never* human. It seems unlikely that we can effectively communicate with them or live harmoniously with them.

Spirits come and go freely in the nonmaterial world that exists just a breath apart from our physical world. In the thin web between their world and ours, spirit traffic intersects like a busy subway station. Occasionally someone from our world, such as Louis, for instance, enters this space between their world and ours. At other times spirits glance longingly at our world on the other side and try to slip through the cracks to join us. These are not deceased people who have trouble advancing from this physical world. These are other spirits who have chosen to invade our physical space and interfere with innocents that they find interesting. Often they are dark spirits.

Helen had warned me that I might encounter human-formed energy beings that would appear like dark clouds of negativity. These, as we know, were generally thoughtforms that had been fed negative energy from emotional outbursts by people who had inhabited that house and fought a sort of invisible psychic war. Most people often fail to realize that their thoughts—whether positive or negative—can shoot like arrows through the sky at a target and assume form. If they are fed with negative thoughts that are similar in nature to forms aimed in the same direction they may continue to grow.

If the thoughts are negative this growth can assume grotesque proportions and hang over a room like a dark rain cloud filled with depression and despair. Only the people who have created these negative thoughtforms can effectively dismantle them by ceasing to feed them. Other people encountering these dark thoughtforms might choose to move away from them, given that they are not of their own making and thus are difficult to banish.

After I had unsuccessfully attempted to remove the dark spirit from Tracy's trailer in the woods, it occurred to me that perhaps I had encountered a negative thoughtform. But this dark spirit appeared to be much more than a dark cloud of negativity. It was cunning and could assume different shapes. It caused destruction. It could strangle people—or try to. Sometimes I could see it, while other times it could effectively hide its presence from me. It was some other kind of spirit, and it proved to be much more than I could handle on my own.

I could, of course, complain that I had not properly outfitted my toolbox with the right tools, and I will also admit that the holy water I used had never been officially blessed by a priest. However, it had been purified with a crystal to cleanse and energize it and had sat overnight in the moonlight. That should have made the water potent enough to do the requisite job.

Likewise, the seven-inch penny nails that I used as spikes and drove into the ground in the four cardinal directions, calling on the watchtowers of the four corners as I did so, should have proved sufficient to shield a building from spirits. I do confess that I did not audibly invoke the watchtowers. Similarly, the kosher salt around a haunted building should have proved sufficient to guard the property from the spirit intruder by forming a continuous line of salt around the shielded property.

My conclusion is that some spirits are too dark and dangerous to banish effectively. We have no effective way to communicate with them because they are not of our world or in any way related to our world. They don't belong here and have entered our world only to cause trouble. They seek light and life, which they do not have. They envy our lives and what we have. They do not come here in peace. They come here most likely to disrupt *our* peace.

I speak in generalities, because we simply do not know what these beings are. There are good, practical reasons why people who study high magick use great caution in summoning spirits. Magicians cannot always accurately predict who will cross over and whether they can control these forces once they do cross over into our physical realms. So the most practical of high magicians will satisfy themselves by simply assuming archetypes of various god forms or dynamic forces rather than summoning actual fire-breathing spirits into their circles.

I recall a fellow I knew at the Theosophical headquarters in Illinois, a young man who followed the esoteric mysteries and tried to establish contact with the spirits beyond our physical world. We cautioned him against it. As I recall, he wanted the guidance of an ascended master in this endeavor. What crossed over when he attempted to summon such a master, however, was something much darker and definitely unfriendly. This Midwest man went mad after the encounter.

At one time people referred to the summoning of spirits as the dark arts or left-handed magic because this type of magic sought to control power through other outside forces. Today most people who study the ancient mysteries and ancient wisdom of esoteric knowledge avoid such sidesteps into the spirit realm as it can definitely become a ride on the wild side.

I have written this book, an account of my own attempts to deal with haunted buildings, not to entertain you. I have written this book to caution you about the pitfalls and dangers of getting too involved in this type of work. Spirits can be dangerous, even deadly, as my friends Tracy, Todd, and Missy discovered.

We can debate what the spirit in Tracy's trailer really was. Frankly, I do not know. What I do know is that I do not want to return to that burned-out mobile home to investigate any further.

My best guess is that my friends on Mount Hood encountered a demon that disguised itself from time to time as a ghost of a little girl. But it also appeared to me as a grotesque, evil spirit, and it didn't behave like the spirit of a dead little girl. There may be other possibilities, I realize, for no doubt there are gnomes or other nature elementals in an old forest like the one that surrounded the trailer. When considering the deceitfulness, cunning, meanness, and savage destruction of the spirit in Tracy's trailer house, I think demon.

Whatever it was, it certainly acted demonic, from my point of view.

If a spirit has entered your world and will not leave when ordered, you probably have more than you can handle on your hands and should back away. You will find yourself out-matched. There is no reliable way to validate the authenticity, validity, and intent of spirits who come into our world via a medium or channeler. We have only their words, as filtered through the channeler, and these words can be deceitful. Once set free into the physical world, these spirits could do much more than merely speak through the person they are channeling through.

Removing harmless spirits from a haunted house by kindly communicating with them and helping them to see their way out of this physical world that seems to trap them is a worthy goal, of course, and probably necessary. However, in other cases I've come to believe that we shouldn't attempt to contact ghosts of deceased people, because doing so may be self-serving. In some instances people might want to summon the spirit of a deceased loved one whom they miss desperately and feel that they can't live without. Or they will want to ask them something that they were unable to ask when that person was alive and well. On other occasions people seem interested simply in chatting with someone who has left us.

Our intrusion into the spirit world to summon the dead for a chat doesn't appear to be confined to loved ones, friends, or relatives. Some people call upon the spirits of famous or glamorous people whom they never met in the hopes of badgering them into granting them a private audience. In my opinion, unless the spirit needs help moving on, there should be no ongoing contact with spirits of deceased loved ones, because their eternal spirit needs to be free to continue its soul's journey. This is true no matter what religion or philosophy you follow.

This sort of pestering of the spirits of the dead has been going on for some time now. It was very popular in the early years of the twentieth century for groups of people to perform séances, whereby a medium with alleged psychic powers would summon the spirits of the dead for curious onlookers. This became quite a circus show, and people like Harry Houdini helped to discourage this practice as a parlor game by proving that many mediums were faking the presence of deceased spirits. That isn't to say that all attempts to call out the dead have been unsuccessful. There are ghost stories that have been thoroughly verified, lending proof that the spirits of the dead can indeed communicate with the living. The real issue is, who is initiating the contact?

Today the practice of contacting the dead has grown far beyond parlor games. Ghost hunters have made their way onto reality television programs where millions of people watch them out of morbid curiosity. It doesn't matter that these onlookers have no personal connection to the ghosts being stalked. Apparently some people's lives have become so dull that they would rather be entertained by the dead than engage with the living.

One program that I, as a pet lover, used to watch was a show where a psychic would contact the spirits of dead dogs and cats for owners who could not bear to let them go. She would make contact with the dead pets and report to the owners what they had to say to them and what they were doing now. Sadly, she would report that the spirits of the pets had not moved on but remain at the side of their owners, sleeping on their bed with them and trailing them throughout the day. Somehow this news seemed to comfort the grieving pet owners on the show, as they wanted the spirits of their dead pets with them forever.

It is sad when we cannot properly grieve for the dead and then let them go. The purpose of funerals is so that we can grieve and, in grieving, properly say good-bye. The ancient Greeks believed that the dead enter a realm far from here (the Elysian Fields) where they can no longer remember the living they've left behind. This is a beautiful concept, because it suggests that contact with the living is properly ended with death and that the spirits of the dead should go through a cycle of change as seen by their melding with nature. Death in this case is viewed as naturally regenerative. In nature flowers and trees die and then recycle into new life-forms. In the Judeo-Christian tradition people generally view the passage of death as a preparation for paradise or a journey from this world to Heaven, which is a spiritual realm separated from our physical world. Hindus see physical death as a doorway to rebirth in a new body as a new person through reincarnation.

One of the great mediums of her day was the nineteenth-century Russian psychic Helena Blavatsky, who founded the international Theosophical Society, which drew Gandhi, Montessori, Steiner,

Krishnamurti, Einstein, and Edison as serious students. The young Blavatsky was a gifted psychic who could manifest spirit on command. As she matured, however, and learned more about spiritual matters after visiting a Tibetan ashram and studying with Himalayan masters, she left this sort of left-handed approach behind her. For the older and wiser Blavatsky, calling upon the dead was inappropriate in that it forced them to return from their natural advancement by drawing them back to the Earth and a life in the past. To Blavatsky, not only was this cruel, it was also a crime against nature and the divine plan for spiritual evolution.

I do not claim to know exactly where our consciousness as pure energy goes after our physical death on Earth. I also do not know precisely which version of the divine truth of life after death is correct, or if they are all correct in part. It could be that there is no real life after our physical death on this earthly plane. Maybe we simply live and we die, as many atheists believe.

I do know that proof of life after death exists. Our eternal life force or higher consciousness seems to live on beyond the physical death of the body. We have reports of people who have died for a brief time and then returned with stories of a different life beyond this physical existence, which they experienced briefly. There are also substantiated accounts of people who claim to have lived before in another time and place, thus lending credence to the idea of reincarnation.

In any event, regardless of how life after death plays out, we should respect the dead enough to give them privacy and peace. We should not disturb the dead. It is not enough to respect their burial grounds and honor their resting place; we should also love them enough to let them go, free of us and this world.

This might be easier said than done. I confess to having consulted a psychic once in order to establish closure with my dead cat who had been run over by a tractor and killed on the farm I had found for her as a supposedly safer place to live. The psychic told me that of course she was okay. She was no longer afraid, anxious, unhappy, or sick. She was beyond all of that. I now feel that my contacting her after she had passed over was terribly selfish, given that I was bothering her at that point. She was over me and ready to move on.

12
Some DOs and DON'Ts for Ghost Hunters

I wanted to leave a little room here at the end of this book for some *do's* and *don'ts* about de-ghosting houses, as my mentor Helen called it. If I had to sum up the whole enterprise in a single word, I would be tempted to simply say *don't*. The ordeal can become difficult, complicated, twisted, messy, and even dangerous.

But that might be a little hasty. Thus, after having "raised" the dead in this way, I agree with Blavatsky. We should leave the dead well enough alone and attend to our own affairs instead. However, I know many of you out there are going to probably try to contact the dead anyway, even if I tell you not to. Also, on occasion, I'll admit there may be a real need to go into a haunted building where the spirit of a deceased person lingers in order to nudge the spirit to leave, given that their presence may be bothering the people who live or work in those buildings.

So *do* help people who report what sounds like a genuine ghost haunting. Bring a hammer and four large stakes to pound into the ground around the building at the four corners, as well as kosher salt and holy water (try to ensure that it has been blessed by a priest!). A mirror might be a good idea as well.

The most important things you need to bring with you, however, are common sense and the ability to concentrate. As you clear the building and ground yourself in order to focus, you will need to really tune in to any spirits that might be present. Do not expect them to jump out in front of you or call out your name. You will be working without eyes and ears essentially, relying only on your inner ability to clear your mind and tune in to your higher consciousness and intuition in order to detect a spirit's presence. Not everyone can do this easily, and for most people it takes a fair amount of practice to master.

On the other hand, *don't* rush to contact the spirits of dead people who have demonstrated that they present no real threat or could probably leave on their own. Also, *don't* remain on the premises or persist in personal efforts to extricate a spirit when it appears likely that you are probably dealing with more than a simple ghost of a deceased person. There are other spirits out there, and you will want to avoid them.

Following are some basic dos and don'ts to assist you in your work.

DO

1. Do assist people who report legitimate hauntings by ghosts of deceased people.
2. Do attempt to aid confused spirits of deceased people who are having trouble moving on and convince them that it is time for them to go—something that should be easy for them, but they might be resisting.
3. Do clear the area you will be investigating of any and all people and animals.
4. Do clear your head and ground yourself. Go deep within yourself to tap your higher consciousness in order to tune in to such spirits. Center yourself by planting both feet firmly on the ground, establish erect posture with a straight spine, and free

your hands and feet so that no part of your body is crossed as this will break energetic contact.

5. Do use tools of persuasion—such as stakes, salt, holy water, and mirrors—to drive them out of the property if they are completely resistant. A flashlight might prove helpful too.

6. Do bring a cell phone or some efficient means of making outside contact with you whenever you enter a haunted building. Make sure friends and family know what you are doing and make sure they have your contact phone number.

DON'T

1. Don't remain at a haunted site if the spirit refuses to leave and cannot be extricated by using the tools of persuasion.

2. Don't remain at a haunted site if the spirit seems to be more than simply a ghost or spirit of a deceased person or that of a deceased animal.

3. Don't allow yourself to be distracted by ordinary sounds that can be muted or tuned out by you through focused concentration.

4. Don't allow yourself to be clouded in your focused attempts to establish contact and communicate with a spirit with thoughts and words in your head. Clear your mind.

5. Don't attempt to make contact with the spirit without first grounding yourself by planting both feet firmly on the ground, establishing erect posture with a straight spine, and freeing your hands and feet so that no part of your body is crossed to break energetic contact.

6. Don't forget to bring tools in case the spirit is unwilling to leave on its own. (See above list of suggested tools to bring.)

7. Don't risk your own safety or the safety of others if you feel that there is a malevolent spirit present who is capable of violence toward you or others.

8. Don't be too stubborn or proud to admit that you cannot remove a spirit from a haunted building.

9. Don't forget to notify someone from the outside as to where you are and what you are doing, and don't forget to bring a cell phone in case you need to call for someone to come get you.

If you have the natural ability to see or somehow detect the presence of ghostly spirits, then people are likely to ask you to help them remove ghosts from their lives. If you feel reasonably secure about attempting this job, then you probably should assist your friends. Do not feel obligated, but do recognize that you might be able to help them and should consider trying.

An ongoing haunting, after all, is an unhappy situation without harmony and resolution. It is like a broken record that is stuck in a groove and cannot start over and cannot advance. Ghosts of the deceased are doomed to play out each day in an endless loop of mystical ritual that must be very unpleasant for them and the people whose physical space they haunt. Whether such spirits are confused, afraid, or reluctant to move forward, they need to advance beyond this physical realm where their natural days have ended. They do not belong here; people who once knew them should release them freely.

Nothing in this book is intended to minimize the tragedy of the ghosts who are stuck on this earthly plane or the need to help release them to advance. Again, my main intent in writing this book is simply to caution people who think it might be fun and easy to contact spirits. I want to warn you of the many pitfalls, uncertainties, and real dangers that can surround contacting any strange things that go bump in the night. These mysterious spirits might prove to be more than you could possibly handle.

Be forewarned.

Recommended Reading

Dell, Christopher. *Monsters: A Bestiary of Devils, Demons, Vampires, and Werewolves.* Rochester, Vt.: Inner Traditions, 2010.

Gittner, Louis. *Love Is a Verb.* Eastsound, Wash.: Touch the Heart Press, 1987.

———. *There Is a Rainbow.* Eastsound, Wash.: The Louis Foundation, 1981.

———. *Listen, Listen, Listen.* Eastsound, Wash.: The Louis Foundation, 1980.

Harold, Jim. *True Ghost Stories: Jim Harold's Campfire 2.* Charleston, S.C.: Jim Harold Media, 2013.

Lecouteux, Claude. *The Secret History of Poltergeists and Haunted Houses.* Rochester, Vt.: Inner Traditions, 2012.

———. *Return of the Dead.* Rochester, Vt.: Inner Traditions, 2011.

———. *Phantom Armies of the Night.* Rochester, Vt.: Inner Traditions, 2010.

Sagan, Samuel. *Entity Possession.* Rochester, Vt.: Inner Traditions, 1997.

Steiger, Brad. *Words from the Source.* Englewood Cliffs, N.J.: Prentice-Hall, 1975.

Index

apartment below, woman in, 22–26,
    48–49

banishing ritual, of King Solomon, 19
barn, ritual walk from, 21–22
baths, mineral, 38–39
belligerent ghosts, 52–54
bird mutilations, 76–79, 82
Blavatsky, Helena (medium), 164–65
body in the lake
    author's investigation of, 79–84
    chapel in the woods and, 85–86
    identified as Diane Boslar, 90
    lack of answers for, 91–92
    mutilation of, 89
Brightwood, spirits of, 20–21
brother's spirit, 26–27, 28

cardinal directions, four, 53,
    161
cats
    author's, 165–66
    ghost cats, 12–13
    Wizard, the healing cat, 16, 17

cell phone, need for, 169
channeling, limitations of, 162
chapel in the woods
    author projecting loving thoughts
        toward, 98–99
    author's visit to, 86–88
    body in the lake and, 85–86
    catching on fire, 99
    described, 70–71
    haunting the author and, 93–95
    Marshall's visit to, 72–73
    missing sister and, 74, 75, 93
choking, ghost-related, 108–9, 133–34
church in Portland, haunted, 3, 57–69
clairaudience (psychic hearing), 50
clairvoyance (psychic vision), 50
clearing the mind, 115–16, 168
clothes drawers, dumped and rearranged,
    95–96
communicating with ghosts
    Helen (ghost hunter) on, 36–37,
        49–52
    speaking without words, 51–52
    unseen problems with, 161–62

See also phone calls from beyond the
    grave; tuning in
compositor, drowned, 11–12
confused ghosts, 27–28, 168
contacting deceased loved ones, 163–64
crossroads, psychic, 41, 55

dad's final good-bye, 15–16
dangers
    of dark spirits, 4, 160–61
    of ghost hunting, 1, 4–5
    of mirror magick, 54
dark-energy mass
    described, 160
    dissolving, 34–35
    formed by negative emotions, 34–35,
        55
dark spirits
    dangers of, 4, 160–61
    nonhuman, 159–60
    See also haunted trailer
death, beliefs about, 164–65
Deb's pink ribbon, 16–18
decapitations
    birds, 76–77
    body in the lake, 82
deceased loved ones, contacting,
    163–64
de-ghosting houses, do's and don'ts,
    167–70
demons, 162
directions, four cardinal, 53, 161
Doe Bay Village, 38–39
dogs, 107, 112, 144, 153
do's and don'ts for ghost hunters,
    167–70

drawers, clothes dumped and rearranged,
    95–96
drawings by spirits, 147–48
dreams, dad's final good-bye, 15–16
drowned compositor, 11–12

emotional energy, 34–35, 51
emotions, negative, 34–35, 55
energy spirits, 42–43
eye, mind's, 50, 51

faces in the skylight, 94–95, 99
Findhorn, Scotland, 40
flickering headlights, 131–32, 133
four cardinal directions, 53, 161
friendly ghosts, 27–28

ghost hunting
    communicating with spirits, 36–37
    dangers of, 1, 4–5
    do's and don'ts for, 167–70
    questions regarding, 46–47
    unseen problems with, 159–66
    See also Helen (ghost hunter)
ghosts
    author's early experiences with, 1, 7
    author's sensitivity to, 1, 5
    dark energy mass versus, 34
    dark spirits, 4, 159–161
    deceased loved ones as, 163
    deceptive and devious, 7
    demons disguised as, 162
    energy spirits, 42–43
    friendly and confused, 27–28, 168
    getting them to move on, 51–52
    good versus bad, 41–42

harmless, 162–63
hostile or belligerent, 52–54
malevolent spirits, 113, 169
not willing to leave, 5
as ritualistic, 49
unseen problems with, 159–66
ghost stories
dad's final good-bye, 15–16
Deb's pink ribbon, 16–18
drowned compositor, 11–12
ghost cats, 12–13
London hotel ghost, 13–15
message from "The Order," 18–19
my mother's dead brother, 26–27
my Native American visitor, 20–21
newsroom ghost, 8–10
old church in Portland, 3, 57–69
overview, 3–4
ritual walk from the barn, 21–22
woman in the apartment below,
22–26, 48–49
See also haunted trailer
Gittner, Louis (author and psychic)
described, 31–32
Helen as secretary for, 47
on love as protection, 97–98
psychic readings of, 44
trance states of, 31, 39–42, 55
work with energy spirits, 42–43
good-bye, dad's final, 15–16
grieving for the dead, 164
grounding yourself, 168–69
grounds, salting
described, 53
haunted trailer, 123, 124, 161
old Portland Church, 68–69

grounds, staking
described, 52–53, 62
haunted trailer, 123, 161
old Portland Church, 66–67

harmless ghosts, 162–63
Harold, Jim, ix–xi
haunted trailer
author's visit with the family, 100–
112
confronting the spirit in, 113–28
consequences of the haunting,
143–58
destroyed by fire, 151–54
mirror magick for, 124–27
returning the spirit back to, 129–42
salting the grounds, 123, 124, 161
staking the grounds, 123, 161
tossing holy water in, 123
tuning in to contact spirit, 115–16
headlights, flickering on and off, 131–
32, 133
hearing psychically (clairaudience), 50
Helen (ghost hunter)
author's meetings with, 1–3, 30,
47–55
author's questions for, 46–47
on communicating with ghosts,
36–37, 49–52
on dark energy masses, 34–36, 160
on ghost hunting, 3, 32–37, 44
on holy water and salting the grounds,
53
as Louis Gittner's secretary, 32, 47
on mirror magick, 54
on staking the grounds, 52–53

herbal mash, making, 101

holy water, 53, 121, 123

hostile ghosts, 52–54

hotel ghost, London, 13–15

Houdini, Harry, 163

houses, de-ghosting do's and don'ts, 167–70

innately perceived music, 20

King Solomon, Lesser Banishing Ritual of, 19

Lesser Banishing Ritual of King Solomon, 19

life after death, 165

"lightning tours" of India ghost, 28–29

Listen, Listen, Listen (Gittner), 31

London hotel ghost, 13–15

Louis. *See* Gittner, Louis

Louis Foundation (publishing company), 47

loved ones, contacting deceased, 163–64

Love Is a Verb (Gittner), 31

loving thoughts

    projecting, 98–99

    sending to ghosts, 51

malevolent spirits, 113, 169

    See also haunted trailer

message from "The Order," 18–19

mind, clearing, 115–16, 168

mind's eye, 50, 51

mineral baths, 38–39

mirror magick

    dangers of, 54

for the haunted trailer, 124–27

    making of a mirror, 125

missing sister. *See* body in the lake

mobile home. *See* haunted trailer

mother's dead brother, 26–27

music, perceived innately, 20

mutilations, 76–81, 82, 85, 89

    See also body in the lake

Native American spirit, 20–21

negative emotions, dark energy formed by, 34–35, 55

negative thoughtforms, 35–36, 160

newsroom ghost, 8–10

old church in Portland, 3, 57–69

Orcas Island, San Juan Islands, 30–31, 57

"Order, The," 18–19

Oregon pioneer spirits, 21–22

Outlook Inn, 31, 39–40

pet psychics, 164

phone calls from beyond the grave

    author's brother, 28

    East Indian author, 28–29

    Laura's missing sister, 74–75, 83–84, 91, 93

pink ribbon, Deb's, 16–18

pioneer spirits, ritual walk, 21–22

Portland, old church in, 3, 57–69

problems with ghosts and hauntings, 159–66

projecting loving thoughts, 51, 98–99

protection, love as, 97–98

psychic crossroads, 41, 55

psychic hearing (clairaudience), 50
psychics, pet, 164
psychic vision (clairvoyance), 50

ribbon, Deb's pink, 16–18
rituals
    banishing ritual of King Solomon, 19
    ghosts as ritualistic, 49
    ghosts walk from the barn, 19

salting the grounds
    described, 53
    haunted trailer, 123, 124, 161
    old Portland Church, 68–69
San Juan Islands, 39, 46
séances, 163
sensing the spirit, 50
skylight, faces in, 94–95, 99
Solomon, banishing ritual of, 19
spirit entities, 41–42, 159–160
    See also ghosts; haunted trailer
staking the grounds
    described, 52–53, 62
    haunted trailer, 123, 161
    old Portland Church, 66–67
Steiger, Brad, 31, 39
stereo, ghosts turning on, 18
stories, ghost
    dad's final good-bye, 15–16
    Deb's pink ribbon, 16–18
    drowned composer, 11–12
    ghost cats, 12–13
    London hotel ghost, 13–15
    message from "The Order," 18–19
    my mother's dead brother, 26–27
    my Native American visitor, 20–21

newsroom ghost, 8–10
    old church in Portland, 3, 57–69
    overview, 3–4
    ritual walk from the barn, 21–22
    woman in the apartment below,
        22–26, 48–49
    See also haunted trailer
summoning spirits, problems with,
    161–62

telepathy, 36
telephone calls from beyond the grave
    author's brother, 28
    East Indian author, 28–29
    Laura's missing sister, 74–75, 83–84,
        91, 93
television, ghosts turning on, 18
There Is a Rainbow (Gittner), 31
thoughtforms, negative, 35–36, 160
tools of persuasion
    holy water, 53, 121, 123
    mirrors, 54, 124–27
    overview, 52–53, 169
    salting the grounds, 53, 68–69, 123,
        124, 161
    staking the grounds, 52–53, 62,
        66–67, 123, 161
trailer, haunted
    author's visit with the family, 100–
        112
    confronting the spirit in, 113–
        28
    consequences of the haunting,
        143–58
    destroyed by fire, 151–54
    mirror magick for, 124–27

returning the spirit back to, 129–42

salting the grounds, 123, 124, 161

staking the grounds, 123, 161

tossing holy water in, 123

tuning in to contact spirit, 115–16

trance states, 31, 39–42, 55

tuning in

    clearing the mind, 115–16, 168

    do's and don'ts for, 168

    at the haunted trailer, 115–16

at old Portland Church, 61

    process of, 49–51

typewriter, ghost at, 9–10

water, holy, 53, 121, 123

water faucet, ghost turning on, 14–15

Welches Elementary School, 77–78

woman in the apartment below, 22–26, 48–49

Words from the Source (Steiger), 31

writings of spirits, 18–19

BOOKS OF RELATED INTEREST

Seven Secrets of Time Travel
Mystic Voyages of the Energy Body
by Von Braschler

The Tradition of Household Spirits
Ancestral Lore and Practices
by Claude Lecouteux

The Secret History of Poltergeists
From Pagan Folklore to Modern Manifestations
by Claude Lecouteux

The Secret History of Vampires
Their Multiple Forms and Hidden Purposes
by Claude Lecouteux

The Return of the Dead
Ghosts, Ancestors, and the Transparent Veil of the Pagan Mind
by Claude Lecouteux

Iroquois Supernatural
Talking Animals and Medicine People
by Michael Bastine and Mason Winfield

INNER TRADITIONS • BEAR & COMPANY
P.O. Box 388
Rochester, VT 05767
1-800-246-8648
www.InnerTraditions.com

Or contact your local bookseller